Common Miscon

This book explores the biblical truths in a modern and relevant way...I guarantee you that if you do not read it all then you will miss out on its purpose, the depth of it, the Joy, the humour and the laughter, the seriousness, the diversity that it embraces and it just shows that there is another way, a better way, for everyone and that it is never too late.

Ever asked yourself, why are things the way that they are? Or perhaps, why does this always happen to me? Well, if the truth be told, the distorted world that we live in is the way that it is because the truth has been distorted and the effects of that on society have had repercussions for many years. Likely even before you or I were born, it leaves us believing that the world that we live in is normal and how it should be, the truth is, the world is far from how it should be.

We live in a fallen kingdom with an amazing, wonderful king, all that needs to be done is to rebuild the kingdom with the king that lives with us. This can only be done should we allow ourselves to acknowledge the king in all of our ways.

In order to do this, we must seek him, as it is written in Matthew 6:33 "but seek first his kingdom and his righteousness and all these things will be given to you. "

With so many editions, revisions, interpretations and translations of the bible it can be rather difficult at times to discern the truth in regards to understanding the language used and even more challenging can be the task of gaining from it, the truth. The truth that this world that we live in is far from how it should be. This book has been written with the intention of doing the will of God, Bearing Fruit in plain simple English, in a real way, a way that people can understand and relate to. A way that relates to how many people may feel at times, real people, people that have and do suffer from the effects of this world that we live in not being the world that it should be. A better world.

As Far As The East Is From The West

Psalm 103 Informs us that as far as the east is from the west, so far has he removed our transgressions from us.

Initially, one may think that the reference to the east and the west is meant in a reference to distance, would that make sense?

Perhaps, or perhaps not.

Therefore, it is important to discern the meaning of the reference of "East and West."

In the east, the sun rises every day, in the west we observe it setting each day. Such is love observable in society in many different ways and in many people's lives. It is born, it rises, it reaches its peak at mid-day, it then begins to cool as it sets and then descends and then leaves darkness as it goes, until it rises again, the next day.

However, we are left with some light, In the darkness of night there are stars, shining their light into the vast expanse of darkness for all to see.

Even the Moon itself is a reflection of the sun, its observable Prescence in the night sky is a promise that the sun is still there and will rise the next day. With all its scars, marks and craters of which we see. Proof of the battles and fights where it has been struck, yet it is only seen because of the light that shines upon it from the sun, that which gives, warmth, light and life.

In the context of the "East and West" in Psalm 103, I am confident in saying that the meaning of it is that Love or Jesus, whatever you may wish to call it or him, is telling us how differently he deals with our sin. Sin being

Unkindness, Impatience, Unforgiveness etc. In fact, he deals with those things as differently as the coming, rising or beginning of Love is than the Going, ending or descending of it.

When people do something that is, wrong, sinful, unkind or impatient, Love forgives because that is who he or Love or Jesus is. When we continue to do things that are wrong, he tries to teach us that there is a better way to live, if we refuse to accept that and we continue to do the unkind things that we do then we will experience the loss of the eternal life that he has for us and experience death or unkindness, unforgiveness, impatience. The things that lead to spiritual death, the death of love. If we ourselves live our lives like being unkind then we will undoubtedly attract those things into our lives from other people, which, can and will make us feel unhappy and discontent in life. There is a way to stop that though because Love or Jesus is patient and waits for us to realise that so that we can realise that we are unhappy and that we are not living our best lives. When we do that, we must repent or stop doing those things and then simply ask for forgiveness, usually from the people that we have been unkind to and sometimes this can be ourselves. When we stop being unkind to others, they to must demonstrate the will of Jesus and forgive without consequences.

If we forgive without consequences then it is as though the unkindness never happened, it is therefore removed from our life and does not cause any problems in future. Although we may still remember the things, forgiving others in this allows an individual to feel happy with their actions and brings joy into their life, it therefore turns what may have been a sad experience into a joyful one. Of course, for an eternal Love or life that lives forever, there is no setting of the sun, there is no darkness to come, there is no death. These are the promises of Jesus that are written in the bible. Is it also that we ourselves could then have the same amazing love and create a wonderful place right here where we can all live forever by rebuilding the kingdom of Love? I would like to think so.

We are after all instructed to not conform to the pattern of this world (the pattern of evil) but to be transformed by the renewing of our minds.

So...does the world or society in which we live reflect one of Love or Christ or does it reflect one of Evil or Anti-Christ?

If you are of the opinion that it reflects one of the Love of Christ then perhaps you are sleeping? Perhaps you are living in a dream, in a bubble so to say. Perhaps you are happy and content with the way things are or perhaps you are blind? Or perhaps you need educating or teaching?

We live in a society that unfortunately condones and promotes activities and actions that bear no fruit at all. These actions are brought about by the Government and those that vote for the government. The Government is also appointed by the Monarch to

Govern the people. Unfortunately, the way in which they Govern does not bear the fruit of the spirit or the fruit of Love, that which we all deserve and would be entirely happy with should we all receive it. Neither does the Government appear to have the intelligence to cut of the branches of itself that bear no fruit, if it does then we are yet to see it. Instead, it appears to continue to reap more rotten fruit and tries to sow the seeds of this which is self-explanatory, it bears more rotten fruit.

If you are unsure as to what the fruit of the spirit or the fruit of love is then it is just this...

But the fruit of the Spirit is love, joy, peace, forbearance, kindness, goodness, faithfulness, gentleness and self-control. Against such things there is no law. Galatians 5 23:24.

Do the decisions and actions of the government create Joy, Peace and goodness? Rather quite the opposite, look at the some of the recent events in society, increases in and creation of new taxes and ways to take money from people.

Instead of taxes being used to benefit people by using them to give people the things that they need such as free renewable energy and to utilise land to grow food for the people that live in the land we see Increases in fuel and food prices and fuel and food imported from hundreds or thousands of miles away at an increased cost. We see people charged to drive their vehicles to work after already having paid to drive their cars on the road in the form of fuel which incurs taxes and also road tax. This creates poverty, homelessness, hunger and as a matter of fact, all things that are anti-Christ, things that bear rotten fruits.

The Anti-Christ isn't an imaginary devil with a pitch fork, a horny tail and horns on his head, it is simply the opposite of Christ, the opposite of love... Unkindness, impatience, unforgiveness, holding a record of wrongs, being envious and as well as boasting in these things, many others.

Look at the Justice system. People who do unkind things that negatively affect others and bear fruit that is not of the spirit or love. Do they receive the love of Christ from the ones that they have caused affliction? Everybody can choose to show and act in the love of Christ to those that have afflicted them, they can choose to teach them and guide them and show them that there is a better way, or a better love.

Or, they themselves can choose to do the opposite and show someone who has been unkind to them their own love, a love or a way that is not of Christ. They can choose to report that kind of behaviour and actions to the police, they may be arrested and charged for such behaviour or face a financial penalty that causes poverty or they may be held in the custody of a prison, in which case more problems could arise because the dependants of that person who are innocent of such things would suffer also. It is likely that the individual will enter a court in the Justice system and be prosecuted and punished for their actions which will undoubtedly affect them for the rest of their life in a negative way both mentally, possibly physically certainly in regards to employment opportunities and as such they may be forced to believe that that is acceptable and that they deserve to be punished and that that is okay and that's just how things are. Those actions lead to nothing more than rotten fruit and the sowing of more seeds of unkindness that will undoubtedly grow into more rotten fruit...those actions can and do push people further away and separate people from living a life of Love, on an individual basis and also together. Those actions cause division, the breakdown of Love, relationships and families and as such lead to people turning to addictions as methods of coping with such trauma and ultimately, more unkindness.

The verse from Galatians 5 23:24 which describes what love is states that against such things there is no Law, so these are the things that we must do. The law in this case can only be interpreted as right or wrong, rules, and that there is no Law or force or persecution for such things.

If we are to build a kingdom where all are happy then how can we ever do this with a police force, justice system and government that believes, acts and behaves in such a way? Surely it must then be accepted that the government that we have is not fit for purpose and if it does not change then must it go? The truth is, should it be told, that it is the right of the people to have a dissolution of such governments should they wish. Meaning that if they do not like what they are doing and the way in which they are governing then they do not have to conform to the pattern of their evil.

Surely, it is not possible for actions that create division rather than Unity to be the Lords will, for it is written in Malachi 2:16 "For I hate divorce!" says the LORD, the God of Israel. "To divorce your wife is to overwhelm her with cruelty," says the LORD of Heaven's Armies. "So guard your heart; do not be unfaithful to your wife."

Is the wife or the bride of every man woman and child in the kingdom of heaven not love?

Are we not joined or knit together in our mothers' womb? Our Mothers Womb being the speech of our mouth. Therefore, are we not all in verbal agreement that these things are true?

Is it not written in Ecclesiastes 4.... Again, I looked and saw all the oppression that was taking place under the sun: I saw the tears of the oppressed— and they have no comforter; power was on the side of their oppressors— and they have no comforter. And I declared that the dead, who had already died, are happier than the living, who are still alive. But better than both is the one who has never been born, who has not seen the evil that is done under the sun.

There are numerous ways of reading the above, in a way where we interpret them at face value where we see sufferings under the sun, on the Earth and also those whose love is not the love of Christ, one that falls short, one that involves unkindness, impatience etc. The kind of love that oppresses oneself by means of feelings of guilt or remorse etc. Feeling oppressed by being subject to evil from someone else can cause you tears and also can the feeling of oppressing yourself because of your own unkind actions. It tells us that this person has seen the tears of the oppressed and that they had no comforter, the comforter being Love, so must be referring to unkind people, in which case, when it next tells us that power was on the side of their oppressors, and that they also had no comforter, where they also unkind? Of course. It then says that being unkind and continuing to be unkind brings more happiness to people than people who are kind and continue to be kind. But better than both of these is the one who has never been born and has not seen this kind of love. In this case it would have been better to have not known division and what it means to be kind or unkind, loving or evil, yet, unfortunately, the speech and actions of many people are examples of how many people have been born. Is there a way that we can be unborn or something like it? Of course, forgiveness.

Forgiveness comes and is needed after a disagreement or an argument that causes division. In the instance of the given scripture, it is as though Love is giving us a message that it is better to have not argued than it is to have argued.

How is it possible to do that?

Through finding solutions, solutions that benefit all!

I have wept at all the oppression that takes place under the sun and I myself have been oppressed, I have done this on my own and the Love of Jesus has comforted me, it gave me a greater, deeper and more powerful understanding of Love. I was born. It allowed me to be rebuilt in my mind even stronger in the Love of the Lord so that I could see things differently. But I am still not yet complete and do not feel whole, I feel the need to give forgiveness to certain individuals but have not had the opportunity to do so.

I see people and their actions and their deeds by the fruit that they bear, I am able to discern who is dead and who has already died, the living who are still alive. I know that it is better than both of these for someone never to have been born, who has not seen the evil that is done under the sun. I cannot help the fact that I have been on the Journey in my life that I have been, I cannot help the fact that I received ungodliness for carrying out the righteous works of the Lord as he instructs. I can not help that through death I was born and that the place in which I was before knowing that the dead who had already died are happier than the living who are still alive. I cannot help the fact that my life was taken away from me by the dead and was stolen and the lives of many others, I can choose to put those things behind me though and keep moving forward, albeit with so much pain because forgiveness has been cut off by evil.

I believe and hope for a reuniting of that place, not just for myself but for everyone, everyone that ever was, that is and that will be, forever.

That place that I call, and truly is...Home.

If we can not build that place here on Earth right now for ourselves or for our future generations then perhaps things will never change and this place will never be home for me or anyone that lives here, for as far as I am aware, there is still death. Perhaps I am wrong and this is all just a temporary experience and the place called home where we came from is the place to which we return and none of this really matters? Would I then myself be living in a bubble? That may be so, but with no factual, tangible evidence to suggest that and no truth to back that up, would I be believing a delirious lie? The truth is that I quite possibly would be. Would it be a good idea to change and rebuild society so that the outward perception of Love is one that reflects the inward? Can we gain that perception of love from the bible? Would it be a good idea to do so? Of course, it would, for it would make the time spent here by others more happy, joyful and peaceful and a much nicer world to live in. What would a bible be doing here in this reality if it was not to be used in this reality?

So that is what needs to be done...not just by myself but for and by everyone who is able.

So how do we or should we deal with unkindness, we should deal with it with kindness and the truth so that it may be guided and taught and shown the better way, we show offer forgiveness.

The Church

I am going to church today!

No, you're not! You are going to a congregation, an organised meeting and gathering of people.

I am going to the roman catholic church today!

I am going to the methodist church today!

I am going to the Pentecostal church today!

I am going to the church of latter-day saints today!

I am going to the mosque today!

I am going to the temple today!

No, you are not, you are going to a gathering of people in a building, people that identify as those types of people. People whose beliefs and ways affect and control their behaviour in one way or another. A place where the leader of such a congregation has an ideology that they can only obtain by the support of others, both by means of numbers in the congregation and more than likely financial offerings.

If you agree with their ideology and don't mind contributing to that financially and they bear fruit in accordance with the Lord then hey, why not give to that wonderful cause?

But is it the cause of Jesus?

Which pope, priest, pastor, bishop, saint, deacon or person of any other title has ever bore loving fruit that has changed the world for everyone and made changes to the way in which people all over the world live life in such a way that it bears loving fruit for everyone?

As a matter of fact, which monarch, president, emperor or prime minister has ever been able to do such things?

In fact, every living person can be a priest should they so wish. For being a priest is for someone to go to God on behalf of others. This is done so by bringing the love of God to others who are struggling and have problems through the teachings of Love in the bible, so that others may learn and also bear fruit. That being so, should not everyone read their bible and embrace the love that is there for us on each page of such a wonderful book?

Again, it is important to know what bears fruit and is the will of God before teaching others so that they are not led astray and so that lies and false teachings are not prevalent in society, which is why society has so many problems caused from division as it does today.

That being so, the Roman Catholic church with its pope and its priests, the more modern church with its pastor and its flock, the mosque with its Imams and Sufi's. The temple and its Pujari and Guru, the synagogue and its Rabbi and Cantor. Are they doing the will of God?

Is not the will of God for every individual to do that on a personal basis? Is there not enough bibles printed on the planet for every living person to have one each?

Should we not all be Priests, ones who go to God or Love Or the bible to bring the fruits of the spirit and enlightenment and peace and Joy into others' lives on an individual basis with everyone that we meet?

God or Love hates division for with division there is a breakdown of unity, the very thing which I am pretty sure that the ideologies of all the above wish for but have never been able to accomplish, unity for everyone on earth.

That being so, do they not see that their individual ideologies and identities, ways and conformities to certain things are indeed causing division? Sadly, be it with all the best intent, they are destined for failure.

Why? Because they are ministering to and delivering the message to the wrong people. The individuals that they see on the street that they minister to and that they welcome to their congregation likely do not have the power or role to change such things. It is the members of the government, the politicians that have the ability to do such things. How many organisations seek to minister to these individuals?

So, what is the answer to these problems?

If it is the hopes and beliefs and dreams of every living being for the fruit of the spirit to be in their life and everyone deserves such things then we should be doing things that exemplify that? So that what we see and do in society each day becomes a pleasure for everyone and so everyone will be eating and drinking from such fruits so that their soul may be satisfied?

....

"There is a new church started that is opening next week, shall we go?"

The above quote is a common misconception of the church and words of a mind that has been misguided and someone that needs to be taught. They would be referring to a congregation of people, likely at a building or premises and likely a group or gathering that is rather more likely to be a business than a church.

So, what is a church?

We are all churches, you, me, your nan, your mam, your dad and your gran. We are the church!

We were all once fully functional perfect churches. Through time and the daily interactions with others and occurrences in our social environments our church can become damaged and need repair.

A rather humorous joke that was brought to me by non-other than Miss T. went as follows...

Back in the days when people had landline telephones and the numbers were stored in a book that was freely distributed and became smaller and smaller over the years, Miss T used to randomly pick a number from out of the book and dial it. When the recipient of the call answered the telephone they would be asked "hello, is this Mrs Walls?" to which the reply would be "no", Miss T would then ask "well is Mrs Walls there?" to which the reply would likely be "no, have you dialled the correct number?"

"Miss T would then ask the question "well is there any Walls there?"

The reply would then almost certainly be "No"

To which Miss T would then ask "so if there is no Walls there then how does your roof stay up?

I imagine at that point there would be a loud laugh or the phone would be hung up.

I pondered and mulled over this for a while... a church without walls! That being so, how does the roof actually stay up?

Well of course, it wouldn't have walls, it would be held up with pillars!

Walls keep people out and also protect people that are inside of them. Similarly, life experiences can allow us to build walls with other people that have hurt us, but that shouldn't be the way. if we hold secrets and have done unkind things to others, we may not wish to have others know about those things because of the shame that is associated with those things and that can destroy a person if left inside if they are not able to deal with such things with love and also build walls with others. Shame is not something someone feels if they have done something that causes them to feel bad. That person would associate with guilt and remorse. Shame is something that is given to an individual who feels remorse by an unkind person. How many times have you heard someone say "you should be ashamed of yourself?" To someone who is dealing with and feeling remorseful, the last thing that they want to hear is those words. Those words do nothing more than rip a person apart than build them up. They cause people to build walls with others and furthermore, they cause division. They are unkind words that clearly demonstrate that the one who says those words is dealing with anger. When someone says those words to someone who is feeling remorseful because of realisation and repentance of their unkindness (which is a sign of growth in love) the recipient of them is dealing with a person that needs to grow in love.

There are many biblical scriptures about churches without walls and also pillars.

If we have pillars, all can freely enter in.

If the truth be told, unless all people accept that one unkind thing is as bad as another unkind thing, that sin is sin and there is no difference in one unkind thing than another and that unkindness is unkindness. That stealing a bicycle is as unkind as murder, then there will always be churches with walls and there will always be problems in society, social relationships, friendships, relationships and families.

Look after your churches people!

There is a better way.

Do Unto Others

"I don't want to pay tax anymore, why is a quarter of my income stolen from me all the time against my will?"

"SHUT UP YOU LITTLE BASTARD AND JUST PAY IT AND KEEP YOUR MOUTH SHUT AND BE THANKFUL THAT YOU ONLY PAY A QUARTER INSTEAD OF THOSE THAT PAY A HALF AND SOMETIMES MORE! IF YOU DON'T PAY IT YOU WILL BE FINED THOUSANDS OF POUNDS AND MADE OUT TO BE A CRIMINAL IN PUBLIC, JUST LIKE THESE BIG COMPANIES THAT WE BROADCAST ON THE NEWS IN SUCH A WAY THAT WE PORTRAY THEM TO BE BAD SO THAT THE MASSES WHO ARE BLIND AGREE AND THINK THAT ITS GOOD TO PAY TAXES AND THAT ITS OKAY TO PUNISH PEOPLE THAT DON'T PAY THEM AND TO TARNISH THEM AS CRIMINALS!"

(EVEN THOUGH THAT'S WHAT THE PEOPLE WHO COLLECT THE TAXES DO ANYWAY!)

Well, that was an interesting conversation, wasn't it?

Unfortunately, it's the truth of how society is today and we see it happening all the time. How many times when taxes are involved have you heard the words "Render unto Caesar that which is Caesars!"

Does rendering unto Caesar what is Caesars or paying taxes in excess, as they are today produce fruits of the spirit and fruits of the spirit for everyone?

Far from it! Ask someone who earns the average wage, are they happy giving twenty percent of their income to a government that produces something that they do not want. Ask the person who earns an income that is over £51,000 and is classed as a higher tax bracket are they happy giving forty percent of their income for the same thing, the likely answer would be no. Ask the same people, does paying that income tax and then having to pay much more in other taxes bring joy peace and happiness into their life? The answer will almost certainly be, no! Therefore, taxes do not bear the fruit of the spirit and are therefore they are not the work of God.

We are instructed to "Watch out for false prophets. They come to you in sheep's clothing, but inwardly they are ferocious wolves. By their fruit you will recognize them. Do people pick grapes from thornbushes, or figs from thistles? Likewise, every good tree bears good fruit, but a bad tree bears bad fruit. A good tree cannot bear bad fruit, and a bad tree cannot bear good fruit. Every tree that does not bear good fruit is cut down and thrown into the fire. Thus, by their fruit you will recognize them. Matthew 7 15:20.

To cut them down and throw them into the fire...wow that is powerful.

So, what would be a good way to utilise the "Render unto Caesar that which is Caesars?"

Well in an ideal world, everything would be free for everyone and there would be no more need, want, pain or suffering and death or unkindness would certainly be swallowed up!

There would be no more need for Caesar should that ideal world exist as there would be no need for money, a truly cash free society. Not just cash free with the use of digital currency but a cash free society without currency at all, one built on kindness.

But as long as we have money and currency is it possible to use it in a way that bears fruit of the tree of life?

Well if everyone was honest when it came to money and decided to not be greedy then Of course, there is, and that is to make everybody Caesar...

The production cost of a typical £80 shirt is just £8. Covering materials, labour and transportation, with manufacturing usually taking place in Asia.

$$8 \times 8 = 16$$

20% of 16 = 3.20

Total £19.20

10% of 19.20 = 1.92

Total £21.12

If the cost of manufacturing is £8 then the manufacturing people can double their costs in order to make two more and their business can double because they can make two more items to sell.

If they charge 20 % of this cost for their wages then they make £3.20 per shirt as wages as well as doubling their production. After producing two more, applying the same principles they will have £6.40 as wages and the funds to produce 4 more shirts.

If 10% of this figure is £1.92 and this is collected for good causes also known as taxes then as people's businesses grow, they get to earn more money, more money is available for good causes, people are happy because they are then able to afford a shirt at £21.12 instead of £80 and if the money for good causes is used correctly then society will be a much nicer place to live in.

More football shirts would likely be sold and the profits would likely be the same.

More jobs would likely be created and manufacturing and innovative ideas would likely increase.

People would be happier, more active and energetic and almost certainly a lot healthier.

Instead of giving 20% to Caesar the geezer (AKA THE TAX MAN) doesn't it make sense to make everyone Caesar given the above? The same with the farmer who grows the coffee beans, the same with the man that transports them, the same with the coffee shop that serves the coffee. Wouldn't it be great if people were able to do things that they enjoyed and brought joy into their life in such a manner?

And if everyone was to give an extra ten percent on top of the cost of something they buy and that ten percent was passed onto the business owner and staff directly then how much faster would people be able to have more and a better quality of life.

I would say the same with the landlord that rents out the property to the coffee shop business owner but with rents as high as they are, due to mortgages, greed of landlords making profits instead of showing kindness and the way that the banking system has made them it may prove problematic. People deserve to own their own places and properties.

Some things may cost more this way, some things may cost less but long term, there are great benefits to this principle.

The key to unlocking love, life and the fruits of the spirit is to take actions that benefit everyone, wouldn't this do just that?

And so, it certainly is a common misconception that people should be happy to pay taxes and live the way that they are forced to with the fruits of the tree of knowledge of good and evil rather than the fruits of the tree of life.

Do we agree?

All that people need to do is to not conform to the pattern of evil. All that people need to do is to say no and to cut off the branch that does not bear fruit of the spirit. To tend the vineyard, become gardeners and arborists. As a carpenter would could cut away any unwanted pieces of a log to carve a beautiful sculpture, should people not become carpenters?

In biblical scripture, who was a carpenter? Can we not all choose to do that on a personal basis? Has our god given right to do that been taken away from us by the rules of society and a Government of Anti-Christ values and ways?

Should they not cherish the work that they do in doing these things and show and teach others the way sowing seeds after tilling the soil so that in future other trees of life may grow and flourish so that we may all consume the fruit of the spirit?

The truth, may it be told, is that unless we focus on building and restoring the Kingdom of God and focus our efforts and resources on that aspect of society then there will always be a need to teach because there will always be the fruit of the tree of knowledge of good and evil until that tree is completely cut down and it is taken up by the roots and cast into the sea. It can be taught that there is a better way and shown that. If it does not accept that then it must go into the sea to experience that so that it can appreciate, learn and understand that for itself.

Unfortunately, it is written and also true, that the world or evil cannot see the truth of the greatest of loves, selfless love... we are told this in John 14 15:21. Jesus Promises the Holy Spirit.

"If you love me, keep my commands.

And I will ask the Father, and he will give you another advocate to help you and be with you forever—the Spirit of truth. The world cannot accept him, because it neither sees him nor knows him. But you know him, for he lives with you and will be in you. I will not leave you as orphans; I will come to you. Before long, the world will not see me anymore, but you will see me. Because I live, you also will live. On that day you will realize that I am in my Father, and you are in me, and I am in you. Whoever has my commands and keeps them is the one who loves me. The one who loves me will be loved by my Father, and I too will love them and show myself to them."

They Sowers of the seeds of the tree of knowledge of good and evil simply need to seek Love and accept that they have rejected Love in their minds, thoughts, words and actions.

We are told that we will be given another advocate that will help us and be with us forever, the spirit of truth or the love of truth! Jesus then tells us that he will not leave us as orphans but that he will come to us, he is therefore the truth and that love and selfless love, love given unto others by ourselves is the holy spirit or the greatest of love.

We are then told that the world or evil will not see Jesus anymore but that we will see him. This because they did not accept him. Because he is kind and who he says he is, so also will we be and so also because I am kind to others and love others, so will others be kind to myself and others. If we will see him, are we not all Loving? Do we not have the capability do be better lovers? We do!

On that day or in that way or in that love will the world or evil will realise that Jesus or Love (as written in Matthew 13: 4-8 and 1 Corinthians 13 4-7) is in the Father or God or Goodness or Their selves and that God or their selves are in Jesus or love and truth, The holy spirit, the greatest of loves, the love of others, selfless love. We are told that they or the world or evil will be loved by his father and that they will be loved also and will show love to them.

Is it not written For God so loved the world or people that do unkind things, that he gave his only begotten Son or love, that whosoever believeth in him or in this selfless love should not perish, but have everlasting life. The one or person that dies unto one self by the giving of selfless love that bears fruit, the greatest of love, the Holy Spirit, to give one's love to another, to bring peace by humbling oneself in the face of adversity. In doing that, we need to make our love the love of Christ, the love that is written in and described in the bible.

The truth, that in order for love to grow and things to get better, some branches need to be cut off so that on a personal and individual basis we may bear good fruit to others so that in turn they may also do the same. We should instruct with love and truth so that others may see what is good and may also know the Father, God.

Evil or unkindness should never be forced upon others and the cutting off of branches that are bearing fruit is never an option and should never be done, for in doing so, does nothing but create a rod for the back of the person that does so. You wouldn't cut out of your own life something that was bearing fruit of the spirit or make yourself do something in your own life that gave rise to unkindness would you? And so, it must never be done to others, by anyone, and if this is done by anyone then it certainly is not the will of God, for is it not written, "do not wake love until it so desires?"

Let's face it, the truth, if it be told is that somewhere along the line at some point in time someone interpreted the bible with a mind of greed and self-gain, perhaps it was Caesar himself? Who knows? Perhaps he did this with the best intentions, or perhaps with greed. Regardless, we are still living with the consequences of someone else's unkindness in society today. Perhaps that person was a politician, a ruler, a priest, a pope, an emperor of a king, it certainly wasn't Jesus that interpreted it though, of that, I am sure.

The interpretation of the bible in this instance however, after many years has proven to be unsuccessful and problematic as we still have many problems in society today that are caused by and directly associated with this.

There is a better way and with that in mind there is no better time for change than immediately.

Jesus was put to death on a cross

Was a man, a human being, someone who was actually called Jesus, nailed to a cross with nails through his hands and feet for the public to see and left there to die?

If the year now is 2023, did this really happen 2023 years ago? Can anyone that is alive today say that that happened and they know so because they saw it happen? I presume not. I am not saying that it didn't happen but simply that I was not there so I can not say whether or not that truly did happen, if it did, it would be a very, very sad thing to have happened, not just to Jesus but to anybody.

So, what does the bible actually say about the death of Jesus?

One thing that I can say about Jesus being put to death on a cross is this...

If we perceive Jesus as Love and the love that is described in the bible and written as, Love is patient, love is kind. It does not envy, it does not boast, it is not proud. It does not dishonour others, it is not self-seeking, it is not easily angered, it keeps no record of wrongs. Love does not delight in evil but rejoices with the truth. It always protects, always trusts, always hopes, always perseveres. Love never fails. But where there are prophecies, they will cease; where there are tongues, they will be stilled; where there is knowledge, it will pass away. 1 Corinthians 13:4-8 NIV.

This love can certainly be killed and put to death, the spear or tongue or speech of an unkind person who does not exemplify the mind of Christ can certainly seek to kill or mute the tongue or speech of a loving person who does exemplify the mind of Christ. If We allow it to do so!

It can be put to death with exactly the opposite of what love is. Patience of one person in a situation can be killed by the impatience of another person. Kindness of one person can be put to death by the unkindness of another person. A person who does not envy could be affected by the envy of a person that does envy. The same for boasting and pride, honour and dishonour.

How difficult is it to be kind to a person that is being unkind to yourself? We see how hard it is on a daily basis, that is why wars occur. One leader will seek to attack one country and the other, instead of saying, okay, come, do what you need to do, will instead retaliate with weapons and a war between countries will start. How many times in the history of mankind do we see a country that is threatened embrace the Love of Christ and trust in it? If it has ever happened then shouldn't these be the things that are recorded in history and given praise to rather than the Anti-Christ events that we do witness? Are these not the kind of events that we see taught to us in the story of the walls of Jericho?

Keeping records of wrongs...now that is an interesting one... an evil or unkind person who has been afflicted by another and would like to see them punished would be keeping a record of wrong. Exactly as we see history recorded today!

A loving person who remembers the affliction caused to them by others would not be keeping a record of wrong but would be keeping a record of people that need to be given forgiveness when they acknowledge their unkindness when they feel an overwhelming desire to want to undo the wrong that they had caused an individual and apologise for it. There is a clear difference.

In society we have a Justice system that does exactly the opposite of the message of Christ and condones and promotes evil, how very sad is that?

We have a police force, social services, Magistrates courts, county courts, crown courts and in recent years councils that do more and more evil. They all keep records of wrongs and in carrying out their actions they make life harder for genuinely good people that have struggles and problems in life, this is very, very sad that they do these things as they are also acting in an anti-Christian way or against love.

We have Judges in courts that on a daily basis cause more suffering and problems in society by instead of serving love, serve punishment and evil to those who need love. Which court in the UK or anywhere else in the world do we hear of, that rather than punishing people, taught about forgiveness and the resolution of certain individuals problems?

It is written that Jesus is coming back to Judge the living and the dead in 2 Timothy 4:1 and similarly in the Apostles Creed it is written which presumably must have originated from the biblical scripture of 2 Timothy 4:1.

So, if Jesus is love and Love can do no wrong because love is what it says it is then what would love give in judgement to an unkind person or a sinner or a person that does evil things? The teachings of Christ, so that they may learn and then live a better life!

Love always wins because love endures and evil being the opposite, does not endure, its light or love rises and fades, just as the grass and the flowers of the field and the wages of sin is death, but the free gift of God is eternal life through Christ Jesus our lord.

The answer is simple, sinners would be given Love in repayment for their unkindness and that would be in the form of forgiveness which is covered in the next chapter.

Yet day after day we see the police force, the courts, social services and now local councils as well as individuals that Judge not with love as from the tree of life but with ways that can only be related to the tree of knowledge of good and evil, once they sow these seeds they rise up and people reap a harvest of knowledge of good and evil and question why things go wrong. They ask why things are as bad as they are and why more and more crime and suffering continues and they wonder why they are not able to stop it...yet not one of them stops and thinks and then decides to read the bible to gain the answers to their problems and they continue to try and resolve issues in their own love rather than the love of Jesus.

How many times have you heard the saying, "you will feel the long arm of the law?"

Many may understand that this means the police force and the justice system etc and that to feel the works of the hand of that arm is to be punished, in Gods eyes it is rather the opposite, he made a way that all may be saved by Grace by giving us self-awareness, repentance, confession and a way to receive forgiveness. That applies in everyone's personal life and relationships with others.

So, was Jesus put to death on a cross? As we explore that a little further in a different perspective of a man being nailed to a cross and left to publicly die, we need to consider first what a cross is and other possibilities as to how we can make life better in society today.   Firstly, we need to consider the cross and what it is, look at the two following images.

A Sword   A Cross

Both objects we see look to be very similar objects, yet both are very different things and serve different purposes.

So which one is biblically correct?

Well, we know that in the bible there are many references to the sword of the lord and as we look at the armour of God or love, something which we all possess, we are able to discern that the sword actually represents the tongue, our words. The things that flow from our minds.

We are led to believe that for a roman soldier the sword served as an offensive weapon against enemies. When sharpened, the sword could pierce through just about anything, making it a very dangerous tool. Rather like the military forces in the world today and police forces that walk the streets with offensive weapons that have the capability to injure and kill people. That would certainly be a worldly, fleshly and evil concept of the sword of the Lord. Killing people and injuring people physically is a very unkind thing to do as I am sure that most people would agree.

Let us take a look at the following scriptures found in the bible.

Jeremiah 47 – 6-7

"'Alas, sword of the Lord,

how long till you rest?

Return to your sheath;

cease and be still.'

But how can it rest

when the Lord has commanded it,

when he has ordered it

to attack Ashkelon and the coast?"

From this we see that someone is asking how can the sword rest when it is supposed to attack?

The answer is this, It is the action of returning the sword to its sheath and giving it rest that does that, in resting there will be but peace and an abundance of it, everywhere. When it is used to attack it must be done so with love, kind words.

Think of a situation with another individual that has been so angry over a disagreement, the more that we entertain them in the conflict with the exchange of unkind words or actions, with a sword of flesh and evil then the more vicious the situation can become and it is like adding fuel to the fire.

The only way to return the fleshly evil sword to its sheath is to stop entertaining the other persons fleshly sword and being still or finding peace and speaking kind words, then will the other person be attacked. If you were so angry with someone and they walked away, you would have no individual to vent that anger onto, it would almost certainly make you feel even more angry and the anger that you had for the other person because you refused to sort things amicably would no doubt consume you and fill you with frustration and then grief, the result of which would lead to your mourning, because of your own actions. Something which you could then learn from. Thus, it is best when a disagreement arises to always be patient, to make sure that the sword of the lord that you are using is the sword of Jesus and not your own spear.

Consider both sides, see which one is the best option and which one would bear most fruit and to see which one would be the correct option in respect of a godly or loving one and one that lines up with the Holy spirit as written in the bible.

Carrying on to when Jesus was put to death on a Cross, we can look at the following...

Matthew 27 45:56

It is a short writing depicting the death of Jesus, nowhere in that passage does it describe a man being nailed to a wooden cross.

The truth, may it be told, is that we can all choose to put Jesus on a cross, we can all choose to speak kind words to each other in all situation, even the worst of situations and we can all choose to nail Jesus to our own cross or sword and perhaps it would be wise to use some epoxy resin and a welder in some cases. Now wouldn't it be a very good thing to nail Jesus to a cross after all? But the challenge and question for many people is, Is it actually possible? It would certainly be extremely difficult to do that in a society that harbours so much suffering and pain. If you care about others and demonstrate selfless love that is. How difficult and challenging is it be a Christian Today?

Wouldn't it make sense to change the way in which society works to remove the problems that cause so much pain and suffering in society and to create an environment in which Jesus is permanently nailed to everyone's cross as opposed to one where there is suffering and pain? Rather than one where people, try as they may, inevitably fail to keep Jesus nailed to their cross? One where we are able to eat of and consume the food of the tree of life?

The book of James 2:12 clearly instructs us to speak and also to act as those who are to be judged by the law of liberty or the love of freedom, to speak and instruct others to say and do things that set people free. unfortunately, we do not live in a society that exemplifies this.

If the way in which society functions has failed for many, many years, time and time again does not work and we are instructed to not conform to the pattern of evil then surely it makes sense to try something different? Something that bears fruit for everyone?

So, if the truth be told, was Jesus put to death on a cross or a sword?

You decide and discern for yourself, see which things bear most fruit.

Forgiveness

I recently read that someone had experienced something involving another person that had caused them harm. Their expression of the incident was as follows:

"I have forgiven people who will likely never acknowledge their need to be sorry, openly defended people who have attacked my character in private and didn't seek revenge against my enemies when the opportunities were clear. It's not because I was unaware of their motives or too weak to fire back. It's because I have gained the strength of integrity and have received mercy at times that I did not deserve it also."

WOW! What a bold, inspirational, positive and uplifting statement.

Unfortunately, it is incorrect, misleading and a lie.

Let's take a look at the first part of the statement... "I have forgiven people who will likely never acknowledge their need to be sorry?"

This is impossible, what is meant is that you have moved on from the affliction caused by others by carrying on with life day by day. Forgiveness is something that is given. You can only give that to someone if they acknowledge that they have done something wrong and that they need to be sorry for that through the feeling of guilt or remorse, then they receive forgiveness and you give it to them. The statement says that the person that caused harm will likely never acknowledge their need to be sorry, if that is the case then they will never likely apologise with true repentance of their actions and it is only by doing that that they can then receive or be given forgiveness, forgiveness is a gift. It is something that we all deserve. The person that made the statement never had the opportunity to give forgiveness and as such they just carried on with life. They are believing in a lie!

They clearly remember the incident that caused them to feel that way when they recall the incident or person that caused them harm and as such, they will still be carrying the hurt from the incident that the other person caused, the weight of which may stay the same, grow or become lighter as each day passes. If the person who caused the harm to the person that wants to give forgiveness and the person that caused the harm did genuinely apologise through recognition of their wrong doing and felt remorse for their own actions then that would change the perception of the afflicted person, the one who wanted to give forgiveness. They would see that the other person was indeed a good person and that they wanted to be a better person.

Things would not just return to normal but become better because that is the kind of thing that people should embrace and that, as difficult as it is at times to allow those things to happen, it actually makes relationships between people stronger. It does this by allowing them to become closer. It promotes growth, growth of love.

The person who made the statement states that he has openly defended people who have attacked his character in private.

Wow... if that be so then that is a very good quality and a sincere and genuine thing to do. They were able to see the goodness in the person that caused them harm despite how it made them feel and still build up the person that sought to harm them. It takes a lot of self-control to do such a thing. It takes a lot to do that in certain situations because sometimes the emotions of how the person that caused us harm can still be associated with how we speak when we remember someone. That is why it is also a very good quality and also very important to be able to listen to what people say rather than how they say it. Sometimes the kindest of words can be said with an angry tone of voice that may come across with feelings of hate, simply because they are still carrying the burden of the hurt because the other person has not sincerely apologised.

Forgiveness doesn't come with punishment and circumstances that were worse than before, it comes with opportunity for love to grow and a stronger bond between individuals. That is true forgiveness.

That is why there isn't as much forgiveness in the world as there needs to be. People believe that they have forgiven people that have hurt them without that person feeling remorse and asking for forgiveness yet that rarely happens. What happens is that people move on from things and realise that separation from the people that hurt them gives them some temporary relief of temporary healing but the ones who caused the pain never receive true healing and forgiveness until they themselves see the consequences of their own actions on the lives of others. Now that feeling of healing is truly immense and changes more thigs than one. It brings freedom.... true freedom, Freedom of the mind, Pure Love! Until that happens, no true healing takes place in its fulness as it is meant to be and unless that happens, we are unable to taste and see the greatness, immenseness, unfailing love that Christ has given us. Neither for the one that caused the harm and not for the one that was harmed, they are both kept in chains, prisoners of unkindness and evil. Forgiveness is a two-way interaction, an exchange of love.

Every believer of Christ must exemplify these actions and processes of forgiveness in order to envisage the true nature of the life that we are destined to live as Christians.

Does not the prayer of salvation contain the words "I am sorry for all of my sins" it is something that we must do in order to be saved and set free from the prisons of our minds that keep us in such slavery.

I have been through and experienced some very traumatic personal events and been on both sides of forgiveness, I caused harm and was truly sincere and apologetic, I was never given the opportunity for love to grow in that situation with the person that I had been unkind to, not necessarily by the person that I had been unkind to but by other individuals that believed in their love rather than the Lords love and thought it wise to take actions that prevented my love, The Lords Love, to grow with the person that I had been unkind to. Some of those people were members of a congregation at what is called a Church. Some of those people were from organisations in society as mentioned previously.

The consequences of their actions and involvement caused division, a great division, one division that led to countless divisions. As a result of that I had to grow on my own, with Love, it came with many losses. The path is never easy. It hasn't been easy for me but I know that my actions were in love and the love of the Lord. If it was never easy for myself to try and join together one of my own actions of unkindness that had caused division then how much more so will it be challenging and difficult for the people involved to do the same with the countless numbers of divisions that they have caused with their unkind actions? Their actions, when I made it clear that they were being unkind and were not the will of the Lord did not cause them to apologise, nor did they see that they were acting in an unkind way. As a result of that hey never received my forgiveness… and so I still wait to give that to them as I would have done immediately should they have realised that their actions in not giving me forgiveness were unkind and ungodly, unloving or anti-Christ. I would have chosen to help them so that they could make things better.

Thay had chosen to not carry on with the path of love, they had chosen to turn around and as such, their love or their roof was upheld with a pillar of salt. We all know what happens to salt when it comes into contact with water or when the rain comes in the storm… and so what will happen to that individual's roof or love or mind in the storm? It will surely, after a while, inevitably fall. They will be back to the place that they were previously, a place where they could choose to receive forgiveness.

The last part of the statement says "It's because I have gained the strength of integrity and have received mercy at times that I did not deserve it also."

The writer states that they have gained integrity and received mercy when they didn't deserve it.

Well, the truth, may it be told, is that we all deserve mercy, the meaning of the word mercy is "compassion or forgiveness shown towards someone whom it is within one's power to punish or harm." We all deserve mercy when we have done something wrong, if we are truly remorseful of our actions and apologise for them. If someone received mercy, that being forgiveness, when they didn't deserve it then to not deserve it they must not have done anything wrong and so what the speaker was saying makes no logical sense. It may be a little difficult to understand and process that if you have never experienced it or applied your mind to it, if it makes no sense then apply your mind to it in respect of a situation in your own life and seek to understand it with all your mind.

The speaker also says that they have gained integrity, the word integrity means "the quality of being honest and having strong moral principles"

Unfortunately, the person appears to have a good heart and is likely a genuinely good person with good moral principles, however they need to learn to be honest with themselves by embracing the truth and seeing things from a different perspective and gaining a deeper knowledge of how forgiveness works. It would appear that by the content of their statement that they are still, in their mind, living in a bubble, separated from the truth by a lack of knowledge, they think that they have forgiven and yet haven't and so are believing a lie because it makes them feel better and in doing so may suppress the pain caused by the emotions and feelings that are involved with the thought of the individual that caused them harm. It may possibly be a sign and cause of or symptom of trauma caused by the hurt that the other person caused them.

What the individual needs to do is to understand how good of a person that they are because of how willing they are to offer forgiveness to the person that caused them harm and that one day, should the time come, they would give that forgiveness to the person that deserved it so freely that the pain that they once carried and harboured, that burden, would instantaneously disappear and that is the forgiveness and actions of the Lord that truly sets people free.

So, there we are, the misconception of forgiveness, it isn't something we give to others if they do not love us. They show us that they love us and are good people by genuinely being sorry, they do this by apologising for things when they were not asked to do so, because they realised that they suffered a loss through their actions.

I have chosen to stop badgering the people that ought to apologise to me for their unkindness. It gave me some sort of release from the trauma, a revelation of the truth. I have chosen to write about it instead, it helps me understand how good a person that I am in the Lords eyes, even though I did not receive praise for my actions by other people, simply because they did not know the Lord. Hopefully one day they may get to read this and have a change of heart.

I know that I did the right thing in confessing my unkindness to others because we are instructed to speak to each other about our unkindness...

1 John 1:9

If we confess our sins, He is faithful and righteous to forgive us our sins and to cleanse us from all unrighteousness.

James 5:16

Therefore, confess your sins to one another, and pray for one another so that you may be healed. The effective prayer of a righteous man can accomplish much.

It is written clearly What we are supposed to do and I did that on one occasion.
The person that I spoke to about this unfortunately decided to be unfaithful and not righteous and instead of serving Jesus or Love to me by sharing my burden as

we are called to do as Christians so that we may take away each other's pain, they decided to Serve a dish of Evil and unkindness by not acting in a Godly way. Fortunately, I experienced the true healing before speaking to them and gained revelation of such a great love.

That is how I know that I am right, I am Just and I am good. God used me to demonstrate his works to others through my life, or did he? Is that not just who we are in our deepest of nature as human beings, before we entered and were born into this world? Regardless of which one is true, it certainly does demonstrate that Jesus is and was with me and will never leave me. How great is that love that it will not forsake me?

That is why I wait for not just that individual but all individuals like that to lay down their own love or life for others so that they may take up the Life or love of Jesus in all situations and then be able to serve Jesus as food unto others, how great will life be for everyone then?

The one thing I do ask is this, how can we give forgiveness to someone or how can we confess and seek forgiveness from someone if they are taken away from us before we have the opportunity to do such things so that we can prevent permanent separation and division. Shouldn't we do all that we can now whilst we have people around us to make things better?

I know that the day will come, it has to do, it is written.

Perhaps they do not because they may fear condemnation for their unkindness, perhaps they do not because they are sadistic, perhaps they do not for they may gain financially from it and may have been overcome with evil...perhaps they are just blind, in which case there is hope for Jesus did heal a blind man.

Forgiveness is much deeper than many people think and yet it is so simple and such a powerful thing because it brings with it such a wonderful thing, Healing!
Something that the world needs.

Healing for the nations!

Healing for the nations, The Holy Grail!

On either side of the river was the tree of life, bearing twelve kinds of fruit, yielding its fruit every month; and the leaves of the tree were for the healing of the nations." ~ Revelation 22:2

Yes, take a look at that wonderful image. What was just a book, once opened, becomes a river, flowing with life or love. A book whose leaves are for the healing of the nations.

And yet another wonderful image with love at its centre, from which all good things flow. The tree of life with its twelve fruits. What if the books of these twelve people where to bear twelve kinds of fruit and the leaves of their books were to be healing for the nations?

Shouldn't this be the Holy grail that we all search for?

We already have the Holy Grail, it is the Bible, we just need to read it in such a way that it becomes Holy, and Holy being loving, loving for everyone!

Many people have misconceptions of the bible and believe that it does more harm in the world than good.

That is likely because the ones who read it had not overcome or conquered before reading it and had themselves misunderstood the meaning of certain things. Take a look at the following...

Revelation 2:7 says "He who has an ear, let him hear what the spirit says to the churches. To the one who conquers I will grant to eat from the tree of life, which is in the paradise of God."

Unless we conquer certain things then we shall never see the beautiful story and live in the amazing love that is written in the bible. It also says in Deuteronomy 30:15 See, I set before you today life and prosperity, death and destruction. If we do not overcome or conquer our own evil thoughts when we read it then we shall never have life and prosperity.

The bible does not cause many problems in the world, it simply highlights the problems of the mind of the individual that reads it, something that they need to conquer so that they can then read the book correctly.

In this instance we have to do something completely new and learn a new skill, we have to listen by reading, unless of course we use an audio bible, then we can listen with our ears as we would talking with someone. Therefore, the spirit is the bible speaking to us and we are the church. We need to do this because what the spirit says to the churches is written in the book of

Revelation and can be found in chapter 2 where the messages are conveyed to various churches, the church in Ephesus, the church in Smyrna and also the churches in Pergamum, Thyatira, Sardis, Philadelphia and also the Laodiceans.

The misconception that the bible has brought about more problems, pain and suffering than anything else in the world is just that, it is a misconception. The truth, may it be told is that people bring about pain, suffering, death and destruction because they read the bible without having overcome or conquered or have turned their face away from it, in a literal sense.

So, what is the Holy Grail?

Is it to live a life full of love?

Is it to be baptised and covered or surrounded in love?

Is it the Mythical bloodline of Jesus as a living person as depicted on documentary shows?

Or is it to seek his life of love that is written all throughout the book that is called the holy bible and to be able to see that?

You decide for yourself, but see which actions bear the fruit of the spirit in doing so.

Marriage

Ah, the marriage, the joining together of two so that they may become one. At traditional ceremonies which may be held at churches, registry offices and other places of worship, the two individuals may say vows and swear to each other the following vows or similar ones such as these.

I, ___, take you, ___, for my lawful wife/husband, to have and to hold from this day forward, for better, for worse, for richer, for poorer, in sickness and health, until death do us part.

I, ___, take you, ___, to be my husband/wife. I promise to be true to you in good times and in bad, in sickness and in health. I will love and honour you all the days of my life.

Or perhaps the following one:

In the name of God, I, ____, take you, ____, to be my husband/wife, to have and to hold from this day forward, for better, for worse, for richer, for poorer, in sickness and in health, to love and to cherish, until we are parted by death. This is my solemn vow.

There are many other examples of wedding vows in which the vocabulary changes slightly, but in an earthly, practical, physically observable wedding, generally, two individuals speak vows to each other as part of the marriage ceremony. It is an exchange of promises or vows.

So why do many marriages end in modern day society and many end in disaster?

One educated guess is that the promises made to each other is the main reason why this happens. It has something to do with the "until death" part.

They promise to love each other so well…. until death. So, when death comes, they stop loving each other, then they have no commitment to love each other and so are free to unleash hell on each other should they so wish, and that does happen. All evils creep into the relationships of married couples towards the end, on many, if not, most occasions of modern-day divorce, many involving money and children.

Exploring death, the death in which comes in marriages between couples in a biblical sense as we move forward isn't that difficult.

If love brings life, then the opposite of love must be what brings death…impatience, unkindness, envy, boasting, pride, self-seeking, anger, keeping records of wrongs, taking pleasure in doing unkind things, not being happy with the truth, not protecting others, not trusting, losing hope, not persevering, failing.

People make promises in marriages to love each other and as soon as they do any of the things that are opposite of love, they have broken their promise and allowed death into their marital relationship and started Armageddon or the beginning of the end.

I know it may sound quite trivial, but in what may appear the smallest of examples allow me to show you an example of impatience, one that quite possibly everyone can relate to.

Two people sat down watching a movie. One person needs to go to the toilet to pee, they say so and as they get up to head to the bathroom the other person realises that they need to go as well and shouts "me first!" as they spring up and rush past the other person in order to get there first so that they can pee instead of just waiting until the other person had been and came back.

That could then be considered as unkind by the person who wanted to use it first. They would see it as unkind because they would have envied the relief of what the other person gained, which was to go to the toilet first in order to relieve their painful bladder, the person who actually got to go first may then boast and say "yes, well I got to pee first didn't I and that's just how it is isn't it?!" they would also be exemplifying pride in their own unkind actions instead of the Lord's should they have initially have chosen to be patient and wait. The actions of which would be considered self-seeking. An argument could very easily arise from this and perhaps lead to anger as emotions and feelings run riot. The person who didn't get to pee first may keep a record of this occasion should it happen again and if it did happen again, they would likely say something like "but you did it last time and got to go first, you're a dick!"

Things like this will affect trust and the next time it happens the person who needed to pee first may just get up and go for a pee without telling the other person so that they didn't get the opportunity to do the same thing again or perhaps they may even choose to lie and say "ill be back in a minute, I am just going to check the door as I thought I heard someone knocking" and then go to the toilet without telling them, this would no doubt cause more distrust because of the lies told, should the other person find out. It is therefore better to be honest and truthful and kind than to tell lies.

Both individuals may begin to lose hope in ever getting to the toilet first and also finding the enjoyable love and peace that they once had in their relationship the first time that they sat down to watch a movie together.

Left to fester without a solution and forgiveness, after losing hope, failure would occur and greater division of their love for one another. Possibly even separation or divorce of their love would occur because they had allowed death into their relationship and broken the marital vows which they swore to each other.

So why do people swear vows? Especially when the bible instructs us not to do so.

If the individual that had needed the toilet first that didn't get to go first had covered their doors with the blood of the lamb or basically, spoken kind words in patience and said "okay then, you go first, I will wait" then death would have been no more and the situation would have been resolved. And after they had had the opportunity to go to the bathroom second, they may then both have sat back down to watch and enjoy their movie.

But of course, being patient comes at a cost, that being suffering, as I am sure that in this case you can imagine if you have ever had to wait for the bathroom with the experience of a painful and full bladder.

So, to alleviate the suffering so that it didn't happen again then a solution would be needed to resolve the problem.

That calls for a different kind of love, a different way of thinking. One of solutions.

Two toilets in the bathroom, an extra bathroom perhaps? The possibilities are endless.

Of course, many things in life that bring solutions come at a cost, a financial cost. If people do not have a lot of money, then they cannot provide solutions and as such, many people will fall into disagreements and arguments and many marriages will end because of suffering.

Those who have what it takes to persevere and don't have a lot of money will likely have a lot of suffering and yet they would have persevered... genuine good people suffering? Is that acceptable or is that something that we should look to change, with Love? Society today is full of problems and there always has been genuinely good people suffering, because of others that do not seek to help find solutions to these problems in selfless love. Those that have the means to help yet do not, is that also acceptable? To them and their love that may be so but that is not the will of the Lord.

It is a rather famous quite that goes as such "all that it takes for evil to prevail is for a good man to stand by and do nothing"

We are all good people because that is the truth, deep down, we are all children of God and yet those that have the power to alleviate suffering, don't exactly do nothing, but they don't do the correct thing. They do what their predecessors do instead of thinking differently and bringing about change, change for the better. Perhaps because they don't know how to because they have never experienced the hardships required to undertake such duties and their pride and views prevent them from doing so. perhaps they have never tasted their own fruit? Let's face it, how many politicians have had criminal records before their roles? Non, because they are prevented from undertaking those duties if they have one, and if they gain one whilst undertaking their duties, they are not allowed to learn from it to become better at their duties but they are struck off and stopped from doing their duties.

Yet who would be better qualified to alleviate crime than one who has understood it and gained from it in a loving way... a criminal?

How many politicians would have had a poor upbringing and understand the ways in which crime is linked to finances and have been in situations where they didn't know when they were to get any money in order to buy food and have no choice but to use food banks etc? I imagine this would be a higher number than those that would have been criminals to be honest but still very low and I doubt that any serving politician would be at a point in life where they would have a criminal record and have to live experience such problems and be able to show empathy for others in those situations and find the solutions to the problems through experience. That, appears to be the truth of the matter, and the list goes on as to why they are unsuitable to carry out their duties.

Yet there are so many solutions to alleviate these problems.

Let's face it, are the people that are making the decisions for millions of people making the correct ones? No, and this is clear because problems carry on or get worse and as they do so unhappiness and problems grow. So, is it fair to say that they are incompetent for their jobs? I believe so.

They are incompetent at their jobs because they likely do not understand the deeper, biblical meaning of love.

And as so many politicians are incompetent at understanding love and they need to grow in love. So do many people that have had earthly marriages and spoken vows and made promises to love each other "until death" when they part. Something that they ought to have done before they spoke those vows. If they did then there would be no need for a marriage ceremony and their lives would likely have taken a different path.

So how do we grow in love and what is a biblical marriage?

We know that many people, because of society and how it has been made to work and function is either taught or learns that its everyman for their self in the world and that this happens because it is a way of life and just the way life is. As such, people see that, believe in that and partake in that, even more so as life progresses with age and people become reliant on that perception. It creates walls!

But if we take that perception away from our minds and ask ourselves, what are we left with? We realise that we are left with something that we have or something that many have had and lost and something that is unobtainable should the correct changes not come about. It is our childhood experience, love, from our mother and father. When everything we needed was provided for us, that perfect love, that innocence.

Innocence being the thing needed to see the beauty of love that we have in our bibles, given to us by the Lord.

It is written in Matthew 19:13 Then were there brought unto him little children, that he should put his hands on them, and pray: and the disciples rebuked them.

14 But Jesus said, suffer little children, and forbid them not, to come unto me: for of such is the kingdom of heaven.

Jesus rebuked the disciples, adults, and called them little children because they had prevented actual little children or innocent people, people of repentance from coming to and receiving the great message.

Jesus told the disciples to not stop the actual little children from coming to him because theirs is the kingdom of heaven, or love of truth about love.

Jesus then laid his hands or works or love or peace on them or gave them his love before leaving.

Therefore, Love and kindness belongs to those who love the truth. We also have the Father, God, the Son, Jesus and the holy spirit, the Truth or the greatest of Loves, that being selfless love or love given unto others, the third heaven, one of three which all interact with one another.

If the truth be told we should all love the truth and so the love of truth or the holy spirit would be the key to unlocking and opening the bible in a way that allows us to conquer or overcome our own worldly, social perceptions of what love or life is and should be about.

In doing so, when we read the bible, we are able to perceive it in the correct way and when that happens, we know and have a better understanding of the changes that must be made in order to rebuild the kingdom that at some point was fallen and which society currently reflects. To change society and rebuild it in a way with Love that best reflect childhood, when all our needs were met seems to be the only solution of growing the kingdom of heaven so that we can all eat from it in a more equal share. We will discuss more on the topic of food and eating later.

But the common biblical misconception of Marriage is this...we are to marry and join together with Jesus or Love in our Minds completely so that Jesus can live with us and then we can live with Jesus and be Love, to one another. Only then, when we are whole and one will we be suitable to live with another, if we live with another who is not whole and we are unequally yoked then who knows where the ox may tread when it Plows the field?

Challenging as it may be, life on our own is sometimes better than living with another in respect of it being more peaceful, as hard as it may be at times. But I do not believe that people are supposed to live solitary lives. Solidarity has its benefits but brings with it so many things that in their self are perceived to be enduring. People are meant to live in unity together. I believe there is a way in which living with another is possible and that would be if they were joined together Love.

Who is anyone but unkind to try and prevent such a beautiful thing?

So, when and where do we learn about and grow in this love that brings about this greater love?

The truth, may it be told, is that the answer is in the mind and through life experiences, a very tough and arduous journey indeed, for some! Is earthly marriage the will of God? Perhaps for some, when they are ready!

Ark of the covenant

Wow! What a beautiful depiction of the ark of the covenant, such a valuable and precious object!

The following two paragraphs are examples of people's misconceptions of the Ark, for those people the Ark is Lost and it certainly can be found!

"For centuries, explorers have searched for the Bible's most sacred religious artefacts. One of the most mysterious of these objects is the famed Ark of the Covenant. The gold-plated wooden chest - one of the most instrumental symbols of faith and God's presence -

was believed to house the two tablets bearing the Ten Commandments. The Ark's exact whereabouts has long puzzled scholars. Where did it go? And why has it remained such a mystery?"

No pun intended but I would have to say that they lost their minds, they lost their love and that they became unkind.

"The Ark of the Covenant remains one of history's enduring mysteries. It's certainly one of archaeology's most perplexing puzzles. Did this gold-plated wooden box said to house the stone tablets on which the Ten Commandments were written ever exist? If so, what happened to it? And where might this legendary artifact be hidden?"

There are also many movies and documentaries available on TV and online that portray the same image of the Ark of the covenant, both of it being a physical object like the one pictured and also something that is lost. How they could portray an image of it if it is lost is beyond me but hey, I do like the realisation skills, they are something to be admired.

The truth, may it be told is that these people, the scholars archaeologists and treasure hunters are looking for something externally that doesn't exist, it simply isn't there.

So, what is the Ark Of The Covenant?

The Ark of the Covenant, also known as the Ark of the Testimony or the Ark of God, is an artifact believed to be the most sacred relic of the Israelites, which is described as a wooden chest, covered in pure gold, with an elaborately designed lid called the mercy seat. According to the Book of Exodus, the Ark contained the two stone tablets of the Ten Commandments. According to the New Testament Book of Hebrews, it also contained Aaron's rod and a pot of manna.

The biblical account relates that approximately one year after the Israelites' exodus from Egypt, the Ark was created according to the pattern given to Moses by God when the Israelites were encamped at the foot of Mount Sinai. Thereafter, the gold-plated acacia chest was carried by its staves by the Levites approximately 2,000 cubits (approximately 800 meters or 2,600 feet) in advance of the people when on the march. God spoke with Moses "from between the two cherubim" on the Ark's cover.

The above text is not a biblical account of the ark of the covenant but comes from a readily available online source and it is very useful, especially when combined with the useful image of the ark of the covenant that has been created by the imagination of Scholars, archaeologists and treasure hunters alike!

Whether this be the correct one or just my interpretation of the ark of the covenant is for you to decide. The truth may it be told, is that this is my understanding of it...an understanding of it that if accepted by others will allow for people to demonstrate more self-control in their lives, to be able to understand why things are the way that they are in life sometimes and to grow in love and become better lovers so that they may bear fruit, good, loving fruit!

So, what do I believe to be the ark of the covenant?

The following image is a great example of that I believe to be the ark of the covenant....

The Human Body, which contains the brain or the mind!

The Mind that is also in our body, it contains the ability to choose to eat from the tree of life and to eat from the tree of knowledge of good and evil, we perceive a situation to be one or the other. If our actions are then to feed others from that, either the tree of life or the tree of knowledge of good and evil then they too will eat from it as a result of our actions.

Our mind, or our brain as we perceive it is in our skull, it is in a place of darkness and the only way that light has direct access to it is through our eyes which are directly connected to it. Our mind has the ability to control what we take into our bodies and our bodies output, influenced by our mind have the ability to control what comes out of our mind. So, we need to be careful what we allow into our minds. If we could make things better in society then our minds would be consuming and eating better food.

Our ears, the things that we listen to and the things that we hear are also connected to our minds and affect the way in which our bodies feel and function by what we hear.

Our legs and the paths which we take in life and the places that we go to affect what our mind interacts with through what we see and hear. That in turn affects what we do or feed others should we not be consciously self-aware and demonstrate self-control.

Are the two Cherubim on the ark of the covenant not a representation of our eyes, are the wings of the two cherubim not our ears? Is the box not our mind, surrounded on the inside in darkness and the outside a beautiful reflective golden colour? Are the two wooden poles that it was carried upon our legs?

If the cherubim on the ark of the covenant and their wings were depicted looking outwards as they are on the human body then that may be so. But the wings and the cherubim on the ark of the covenant are depicted as looking inwards.

What does this say or show us?

I believe that if we are to grow and seek Jesus after the world or society has made us the way that we are then we need to turn our eyes and our ears the other way round and take a look at our own minds, we should examine our own thoughts and listen to them. We are constantly faced with choices in everyday life, we can make good ones and not so good ones, we have a choice of two. We can listen to God or Love or what Moses brought, The two tablets. If we listen to what Moses brought then our minds become divided into two. If we listen to what Love says then we bring unity, fulness and completion into our minds and then are able to bring that into the world. We can see the love in life, the fruit of the tree of life and we can see the love in life that could be made better, the fruit of the tree of knowledge of good and evil. The things that require solutions. But what are we doing about it on a grander scale, worldwide, to make things better so that all people can live in unity in the kingdom of heaven?

How canny, there where two tablets of truth contained in the ark of the covenant and yet the mind or the brain has two sides that function separately, or so they say. Perhaps if the same observations were done when one was at peace, they would see different results. Or perhaps they only perceive the brain to be working separately because their minds are divided because of what they are doing, that being so, if their minds are divided by their actions in doing that then should they ought to be doing that? Should they be exploring the mind in such a way, or should they be exploring the mind in the biblical way by reading the word of God?

How long must our minds be divided by what we see and hear in everyday life, how long must humanity fail to take correct actions to make things better?

Perhaps when we turn our eyes inward as well as our ears and we stay still and do not walk, it is then that we are able to enter into our minds, complete darkness, just like a star shining in the night sky, surrounded by complete darkness. As it is when we sleep at night, how peaceful is it when we sleep? Nobody knows because they are sleeping, the peace that comes from it therefore is so great and amazing that it is not comprehendible.

Now what if that peace that is the inward reflection of humanity was to become the outward reflection of humanity, through works that bring the correct changes.

WOW!

How long before our lives and our minds may be made whole again so that we can all come alive again and be resurrected together for the last time?

Maybe it will never happen, maybe I will never get to live in that perfect place, in which case, if you are reading this then the likelihood is that neither will you.

I dread to think what things may be like in future for those who come after us should things not change. And after all of my experiences in life, I still have a hope for a better future, not just for myself but for everyone.

So, the Truth, May it be told, is that the Ark Of The Covenant may really exist after all, it may not be lost after all, and there may certainly be a way of finding it for those that seek it and those that believe it to be lost!

Perhaps it was found a long time ago by Indiana Jones, was he not a raider of the lost ark? You bad, bad man for keeping all your treasure from the ark to yourself instead of using it in a way that everyone had access to it!

(That just made me chuckle!)

For any readers that do not know, Indiana Jones and the raiders of the lost ark is an action movie in which an archaeologist and treasure hunter character enters upon a dangerous journey faced with all kinds of perils and is faced with a vast array of death in order to seek for treasure! Rather like life I guess!

Adam And Eve

God made Adam and Eve, Not Adam and Steve, right?

God made man and Woman and they were called Adam and Eve. The bible says so and so it must be true.

God didn't make Adam and Steve and the bible doesn't tell us that does it, in that case Gay and Lesbian people are Evil and an abomination in Gods eyes, so that must also be true, am I correct?

That being the truth, if it is true, then Gays, Homosexuality, Lesbians, Transgender, They, Them and everyone else that identifies as something other than a straight man or a straight woman that comes under and flies the rainbow flag of the LGBTQWERTY….OH FUCK IT, LETS JUST CALL IT THE ALPHABET FLAG!

Those individuals must not have been made by God and they must be wrong in their beliefs and as such must be the opposite of God and therefore Evil and unkind and impatient and hold records of wrong etc. That must surely be true, mustn't it?

I'm not playing Eve here by asking a question and sowing doubt or anything and wouldn't wish to lead anyone into temptation by saying "but did God say this?"

I am simply saying what God actually said.

God made Man and he made woman, two very different words and two very different things.

Again, we have stumbled across the number two again, as there were "two" tablets of stone or two things in the mind, a division.

Many people, unfortunately have a misconception about Adam and Eve.

What if Adam was to represent the tree of life and what if Eve was to represent the tree of knowledge of Good and Evil and what the tree of knowledge of good and evil came about because of the thing that Eve did? She doubted! Is it possible that knowledge of good and evil came about because of that such thing, Doubt?

Of course, it is very possible and it also is true.

That being so, should we and is it correct and loving and justified to say that Adam and Steve or that Evie and Ivy are evil? I think not!

Now on one occasion whilst attending a congregational service at a building I was "force fed" some food by someone at the other side of the congregation who felt the need to shout out in a moment of prayer and reflection "I can't believe that God would allow for Gays to come into this church!"

If he was referring to homosexual people being allowed to attend the congregation in the building then I find that rather unkind personally.

If he was referring to homosexual people coming into his church or his Body and he didn't like that then I can appreciate that he may think that that is unkind if he was a straight man but I doubt that happened at the time in the service that he was attending, unless of course he was experiencing a homosexual ghost or phantom that was perhaps bothering him, but again, I doubt that that happened at the time that he shouted those words.

Now if he was a straight man and shouted "I can't believe that God would allow Gays to Cum in this church" and was referring to his own church or body and a homosexual person had had sex with him and Cum inside him and they had done that against his will or if he had asked the Homosexual person to stop then yes, I completely agree with the man in shouting what he did because that wouldn't be kind at all!

I Know that because as well as many other things, I have experienced a very similar thing, something that took years for me to process and overcome and something that I am still waiting patiently for someone to remember, feel remorseful about and apologise so that they can receive forgiveness and be unburdened. That is if they should ever feel that way. I know that I would be remorseful if I had done such things.

So, that being so, what does the bible say about Adam and Eve in the bible that could allow us to overcome and conquer such a thing that causes so many problems in society in regards to the alphabet flag?

Galatians 3:28 Tells us, "There is neither Jew nor Greek, there is neither slave nor free, there is neither male nor female, for you are all one in Christ Jesus"

If there is to be neither male or female then Surely God did not make a male and a Female and he did not make Adam and Eve, but yet it is indeed written that he did make man called Adam and Woman called Eve. How confusing, would you not agree? Would it not make more sense therefore that Adam did represent the Tree of Life and that Eve did represent the Tree of Knowledge of Good and Evil? Of course, it would, and if God made those things, then who is God?

Men and Women? This would appear to be a plausible answer, peoples own love, not the love of The Lord but the love of the Son Of Man. And if so, then are Men and women God? That also would be plausible, their own Gods or their own love, Not the love or the one true

God. Is that not the reason why God, or the one true God, expelled them from the garden of Eden?

Each have the ability to choose between believing and doubting and both males and females do at times, unfortunately, doubt. It therefore makes sense that Adam and Eve are simply a depiction of the mind and that which was inside the Ark of The Covenant.

If our actions come from doubt and create unkindness then surely our actions to believe have the power to amend the actions of doubting?

So, the truth, may it be told...

It is possible that Adam and eve are also a representation of our mind and how it works? It is very possible. Is it possible that things in society and everyday life bring us unhappiness because there was doubt by individuals in the past, men and women alike?

Of course, it is.

Is it true that homosexual people and everyone who flies the rainbow flag is wrong, evil and unkind? I would like to say no, that is not true. Not because I live that lifestyle myself, far from it, I prefer the voice, figure, smooth skin and love of a female body rather than that of a male. Who am I to suggest that their actions and preferences of attraction are unkind? Would it be kind of me to do so if they were to take offense at me doing so, would that be the lords will if it were to cause division? Would Gay men, Lesbian women or transgender people be being unkind to me if they were to have sex together? No, far from it and if I was to be offended by it then I would know that there was a problem in my mind that I had to deal with and overcome.

The truth is that Love goes deeper than what we feed our minds through what we see, a lot deeper. It comes from a place called home, a place where it is created, a place where it lives and that place is in the mind.

Close your eyes, pop in some ear plugs, rest for a while and ask yourself, what am I?

I have spoken to and spent time with some of those individuals that fly the alphabet flag and experienced that some of those people are extremely helpful, caring and considerate people. I can not tell them that what they do is wrong or right, I can not tell them that they are loved or rejected by God because of their sexuality. All that I can do is love them. I could share Gods love with a gay or lesbian person and give them a bible. If they chose to read it on their own and were changed by it then that that would be Gods will for their individual life.

But look at this, what if I gave a transgender person a bible, one that had already had the full works done?

What if that person was then to be changed in their heart and realised that they had perhaps shouldn't have had the full works and gone through all the pain that they had been through in doing so? could they ever get back that which they had lost? I think not, if they did then it would never be the same again. How much heartache would that person then suffer at the loss of what they could never get back? I would never want to go through all that pain.

On that basis alone, how much better would it have been for that person to have been happy with what they had at first and to have treasured, appreciated and accepted it? The same way that we should have treasured, accepted and appreciated Love!

How much more would that person then need to be loved by others because of how they felt so that they could be their selves in everyday life? rather like Eve and Sarah.

The truth is this, so much division has caused so many problems in society but God loves us all. We should accept that which we have now, love it, appreciate it and treasure and without causing anymore division, we should seek the opposite, Unity and marriage.

Who am I if I chose to be unkind to someone for that reason, or any reason at all?

Isn't the alphabet something that we should embrace? Something that has everyone's name covered, the colours of such flag which resemble the colours of the rainbow? Something that people refer to as Gods covenant of peace? Is this not gods will, for us all to live in peace?

Is it possible that God created Adam and Eve as he said so in black and white as it is written in Genesis and that happened a long time ago? Of course, it is and the evidence for that, that I am able to see is all around in relationships and the functioning of society.

Although people, men and women, make bricks and build houses that they live in that fall apart and into states of disrepair over time, although Men And women have issues and problems that are caused in everyday life through choices that are made by them, influenced by others, we have evidence of a greater God that we are able to see without stepping out of the door of our houses, we can see it through our windows. Something that no Man or woman could ever make. A living bird, a cat or a mouse, or any other animal for that matter. The Grass in the fields, the flowers and the trees that sway in the wind. Man and woman, people, have tried to be like him, they have learned to regrow grass and plant seeds to grow trees, they can put animals together so that they can breed and reproduce and a man or a woman can say "look at what I have created" and they can be like god, and that is amazing, that is what they are supposed to do and we know that because god tells us so in Genesis 3:22. There is a difference though, being like God is not the same as being God.

Creating a living animal or a tree or flower or piece of grass from nothing is something that I myself could never do and if I have not yet been able to do it. How great is the God that made these things? The one that I try my best to seek and to speak to and to learn about and to want to understand and to want to live with and to embrace ones Prescence. The thing that so many people appear to neglect at times!

So, as the meaning of the life of men and women is to love one another and make things better by using the love that they have, caring for one another as they would want others to care for them, how can they make things better without knowing the God Of Creation?

The one referred to as Mother Nature, the God of Creation, what a marvel!

The God of creation is such an amazing God. So great, that in their human nature, they seek to understand him through experiments such as smashing atoms together to try to understand the Big Bang, a theory that they have on how the universe began. But look at what happens, they smash two atoms together and they become divided into so many other little pieces. So, just as the people that are able to observe that the brain functions in two parts where incorrect and not seeking Gods will, how similar are the actions of the people that explore creation using science that causes division?

They travel further away from the truth and God in their actions when all that they need to do to explore and understand the God of creation is to read his word and explore their minds, with Love.

We know that works of division are not Gods will, for God is a God of unity, not divorce and separation! I was once whole and undivided, we all where once whole, we were all once children, we are all still children, living with love, not being love because of a lack of love, let's make love, let's make things better!

DO NOT CURSE THE HOLY SPIRIT FOR IF YOU DO THEN YOU WILL NOT BE FORGIVEN!

It is written in the book of Matthew, chapter 12 verse 31-32 And so I tell you that every sin and blasphemy will be forgiven unto men, but the blasphemy against the spirit will not be forgiven. Anyone who speaks a word against the son of man will be forgive, but anyone who speaks a word against the Holy spirit will not be forgiven, either in this age or the age to come.

Now whether the holy spirit be a greater god than men and women and that be Mother nature or whether mother nature be greater than men and women and the be greater Gods than that, who knows?

Let's explore it and navigate this topic with Love!

But if the holy spirit of man and woman or humans in our male and female bodies is selfless love, Love for others, and this be true, then to serve others with a true loving heart and mind and to take pleasure in that so that they can eat of the fruit of love that we bear unto each other is the holy spirit, how can that possibly be a misconception as perceived by another person?

Well, because of impatience, lack of understanding and seeing the bigger picture and a failure to communicate and ask questions.

Allow me to explain...

Quite recently I was visiting a friend at a public house and having some food. My friend worked there, as he finished work, he began to enjoy a couple of drinks with me and we began to chat. I'm not going to lie to you, he had had a few drinks previous to me arriving and by this time he was rather messy but still capable of having a good conversation.

We both were stood at the bar waiting to be served. As the young Bar Lady who was working, with a smile on her face said "I'll be with you in a minute" whilst making someone else's drinks, she mistakenly poured the wrong shot of alcohol into a glass. I noticed and said to her "don't worry about that, we will have it, let my friend drink it." As she passed the glass of alcohol which was a spirit to my friend, I said thankyou and explained to my friend that he had a free drink. What is it he asked? A drink, a free drink I replied.

" Yes, I know it's a free drink but what is it, what is that?" he asked.

I was thinking of telling him that it was Peach Schnapps but instead my reply was "The holy spirit"

To which, his reply, at the top of his voice and in a rather angry tone so that everyone around could hear, shouted... "do not blaspheme the Holy Spirit, you will never be forgiven!"

I dare to think what the others in the pub thought about this but I can imagine.

What my friend failed to see due to impatience, intoxication, understanding and lack of asking questions was what I meant by the holy spirit.

He had failed to see the selfless love of another, the bar maid that had mistakenly poured a drink, who was enjoying her work in serving others and that had freely given something to my friend even though she did not have to do so. It was kind of her to do such a thing and she did so without thinking about it when I asked. She was a perfect example of selfless love for others.

And yet my friend could not see that, whether that be to the intoxication of alcohol at the time or his misinterpretation of the holy spirit, who knows.

But if the Holy spirit of humans is to love others in selfless love, the bar maid, a female, a woman had already obtained that goal by doing what she did and finding Joy in it. That being so, who said that Eve or woman was Evil?

Shouldn't that be the Goal of Mankind, Male and female alike?

So, if the truth be told, the holy spirit is not an alcoholic spirit drink in any way shape of form. I am pretty confident in saying that it also isn't a Ghost that comes to visit whenever it sees fit.

As a matter of fact, alcohol inhibits a person's ability to see that and to those who wish to say and justify their alcoholism by saying "Well Jesus drank wine!" then they also are mistaken.

And to those that choose to accept that Jesus paid the price for all our sins so that they didn't have to do so and use that as an excuse to justify their own actions and carry on doing unkind things, NO, that is not correct. To those people, they are missing out on so much that God has to offer them and have twisted the word of God to find peace in their actions that otherwise would cause them so much pain, many do so in order to cover up or mask pain that they are already dealing with, pain from past hurt and trauma. Things that could easily be resolved with forgiveness, true forgiveness with healing.

Something that I know exists because I have tasted and seen it, something that others sought to destroy by their unkind actions that are widely believed in society to be good yet they can only be attributed to the tree of knowledge of Good and Evil.

The truth, if it may be told, is this, Jesus or Love, is the Holy spirit. If we are to speak a word against the Son Of Man or the Love of Man or unkindness, we will be forgiven. If we will be forgiven for that then are we supposed to do that? The answer is no. we are to speak the truth and to speak the truth in Love.

We are instructed that we should not speak a word against the Holy spirit or The Love of God. If we do then we will not be forgiven. Its that simple.

But hold on a moment, is that possible for us to not be forgiven for doing such a thing, if we were to be so Bold to do so? God does indeed instruct us to be bold and courageous, does he not?

Would it even be possible for God to not forgive us for doing such a thing if we did? I doubt very much that he wouldn't forgive us, for if he didn't then he wouldn't be God and he would be denying who he is. It would certainly bring an end to himself and his Kingdom should he not forgive us. But is it not written that of his kingdom there is no end? Therefore, he has to forgive us and so we should forgive others in the same way, for to not do so creates division or Divorce.

Taking that to a personal level, do we do that in our own lives so that we can exemplify him and show that to others? Many of us do without even realising it on a daily basis. If they did then they would see God and they would see God on a daily basis many times.

Knowing and believing that God is Love, looking back to the picture and the scripture of The Ark Of The Covenant when a Man named Uzzah touched the Ark in order to steady it, we are told that Gods anger burned against him and that he was struck dead or struck him down etc. If God is love and Gods anger burned against Uzzah then what is Gods anger in this context? It simply says that the anger burned against him, it does not say that it burned him. But he was struck down, knowing that, what kind of Love would burn against us but not burn us and strike us down? Does being struck down in this case mean that we are humbled? If so, what does it mean to be humbled? It means to be thankful.

The way in which I perceive this message is this... we all have a mind of Christ or of Love, I know this because the bible tells us so. We see an example here in this scripture of the Ark or a mind stumbling, for whatever reason. We are shown that Uzzah acted in love to steady someone else's mind and in doing so he held out his hand to do so. in holding out his hand was he not shown to be offering his own love and kindness to the person whose mind was stumbling? And in doing that did he not receive Love back by being humbled? We see an act of selfless love here, an exchange of it. We learn that selfless love is to help someone else when we do not need to, if we do that then the reward of that is being humbled or thankful. When we are thankful for something we experience a feeling of warmth and happiness and Joy, the fruit of the spirit! Building others up in our actions of Love also allows us to build ourselves up in love and share in eating of the fruit of the spirit or the tree of life.

Knowing that, we get to perceive God for who he is.

We get an insight and a different message from the bible, we see a different story, the better story, one of pure love and an example of what we are to do for each other in selfless love. But of course, we know that we should be hoping for better things, a life for everyone to live without any doubt, without any pain and suffering and no more tears.

If that is so and we are still here after having overcome such things in life then that certainly is evidence that Love is real and although at times people can be unkind and there is unkindness in the world, we are able to build ourselves up again in love when the son of Man falls as God wants to do. At times, people simply need to turn towards God rather than away from him.

We should therefore only fear the Lord if the Lord is the son of man and the son of man is our own love, for that brings about only destruction and destruction of ourselves and our own minds. We should not Fear the Lord, the Love of the king of kings, the Holy Spirit.

I personally do not believe that we should be unkind to or curse the holy spirit, I do know that if we do that, we will indeed be forgiven for it because the bible tells us so. what could possibly happen if we where to curse of be unkind to the holy spirit and to blaspheme the holy spirit? Would God allow us to do that if it is such an unkind thing to do? We do have free will given to us by God after all, don't we? If I was to do such an unkind thing and it was unkind then wouldn't God let me do that, and if he let me do that then wouldn't it be Good? If I was to do such a thing and it was Gods will then it would surely have to bear the fruit of the spirit wouldn't it? It would have to serve his purpose, to bring joy and peace into the lives of others would it not? If it did not then would those individuals be prepared to make the choice to go on a personal journey by looking in the mirror to understand why they did not find such a thing to bring joy and peace into their life? would they be willing to go on that journey to realise that they are in chains, in prison, the prison of their mind?

Sometimes we miss out on Joy and peace because it is stolen from us because of the way in which think, the way that we are programmed to think, through our upbringing in life and the rules that we are taught and expected to follow. If this happens then we should seek him more so that there be more of him in our environments.

Should we be loved with nature or should we be nurtured? Or should we be nurtured with nature?

The true nature of God?

Selfless Love, the Holy Spirit.

A LOOK INTO THE MIRROR

There Are Different Kinds Of Mirrors That We Experience In Life And Each Serve A Different Purpose. For Many People They Perceive The Mirror To Be The Shiny Piece Of Glass In The Bathroom, Or The Hallway. For Some People The Reflection Of What They See Serves A Purpose. It Allows Them To Style Their Hair On Their Own, Brush Their Teeth, Or To Put On Makeup or to simply see their selves before meeting others so that they can have others see them at their best. How many people would use a mirror to allow others to see them at their worst, how many people would use a mirror to see their own spots and blemishes and ugliness so that they may then go and share that with others, and what purpose would it serve?

For Some People They Are Happy With What They See In The Mirror. For Some They Are Not. The Ones Who Are Not happy with their appearance May Wish They Could Change Their Appearance, Some Of Them May Be Able To Do Just That. The Ones Who Are Happy With Their Appearance. I Am Sure, Have Their Days Where They Themselves Look Into That Mirror And Don't Feel

Their Best. We all have spots and blemishes and inner struggles.

Our physical Appearance Should Not Matter And Should Not Let Us Be Held Back In Any Way. Neither should it allow us to be prevented from loving others. We Shouldn't Look into That Mirror And Feel That We Are Unhappy With The Things That We See, we should see things that we need to make better and we should try to find solutions for that, the solutions that God gives us. Many of us become self-aware of our blemishes and try to hide them from others, we try to cover them up, the covering up of genuine unkindness is also not gods will, that shit keeps us in chains! That being so, why does that even happen?

The Mind!

If we refuse to accept that we have the mind of love and to perceive that then we will struggle. Yet there are ways in which we can rectify those struggles in life, without doubt, we can make life better, for everyone, with solutions to problems that benefit everyone.

The bible tells us to consider the flowers of the field and how they grow, they neither toil nor spin, yet I tell you even Solomon in all of his glory was not arrayed like one of these.

So let us consider these things, from a tiny little seed planted in the soil of the earth, they receive water which allows for growth, and of course, with the help of the sun, something that, without, they would not grow at all.

Are we not all seeds when we are born as babies? Did we not all receive water or life to help us grow? We can only grow through receiving water if we allow ourselves to. But to grow correctly and to the best of our ability we need to receive the right amount of water with the correct nutrients in it, otherwise we will not grow in the way that we are supposed to. Think of that in respect of life and the struggles that we all face, some more than others, some people with not enough struggles and some with too many.

The piece from the bible in regards to the flowers and the grass is meant in one way, but it causes me to think...I like to take that little piece from the bible and look at it on a grander scale, through a telescope!

Mirrors serve another purpose also; they are very useful for technology. Telescopes contain mirrors, they work by reflecting and magnifying light, they allow us to see things that are far away in greater detail. We can see things that normally, we would never see! They allow us to see the bigger picture. Amazing things!

So, that thing that can make the best of people feel crappy on the best of days, the mind, let's go and explore it, let's look to the heavens, through a telescope!

The sun, yes, that big yellow orange ball of fire in the sky, the thing that shines its light upon us each day. The thing that gives warmth to us all, the thing that allows all the plants, flowers and trees to grow. The thing that we lie down at the beach and bathe in because it allows us to feel warm, the thing that we all appreciate and could not live very long without. Well, that big orange, yellowish coloured ball is, as we are told, a star!

Just like the others in the night sky that we can observe. Some of those stars are yellow just like ours, some are blue, some are red, some are white and some are black. Amazing things are stars!

Perhaps I should have started with the nearest celestial object before one so far away, but anyway...the Moon! The moon that we see through the telescope, appears battered and bruised with all of its craters through the impact of things that appear to have been thrown at it from the vast darkness, unlike the sun, it changes from day to day, one day shining its light down upon us with a greater magnitude than others. Some days we see that only half of its light is shining upon us whilst the other half is in complete darkness. It would be wise to remember though, the light that it shines upon us is but a reflection of the sun, the one that allows us to see the beauty of the moon after all of its battles. Even more amazing is the fact that most of the time we only see this beauty of the moon best when it is in complete darkness and when the sun has set and hidden itself. Without the sun we would not see the moon at all, it would be a ball of rock floating around in the midst of space, almost certainly unobservable to the naked eye. In fact, the world would be a pretty dark place altogether and we wouldn't see very much at all. Would we?

The stars in the night sky in all of their great sizes and colours, shining their light so bright from afar, deep in isolation of the vast expanse of darkness which we call space. Colours of red, white, blue and yellow. How are they formed? Why do they have different colours? Why does their light shine brighter at times than it does at other times?

In order to answer these questions, we need to look at and appreciate life without others, as it is around us.

Be it on earth as it is in heaven, as above so below etc

Now the bible also tells us in Galatians 3 verse 28 that there should be no more male or female so please disregard that in the above picture and think of this...

The way in which our minds work and Relationships with other people, the way in which we live life with others, the way in which we live life in society... there is so much PC or political correctness, there is so much "this is the correct way to do this, this way is right, that way is wrong," so much conformity, so many demands and expectations.

Who can meet them all?

We could try, and many people do try, the consequences of which would be to suppress who we really are, it would drain us, tire us out. And it does, life is hard, when there is little Joy!

It takes its toll on the mind and that affects our feelings, our emotions and our bodies and eventually, our relationships with others.

We get battered and bruised, our minds full of craters, our lives full of holes due to the loss that we incur on our journey through life, we are changed, our beauty diminishes. The sad thing is, that the thing that caused those things can never, no matter how hard it tries repair or restore the loss and all those holes. So why do people continue to do it to each other and why do they perceive it as acceptable to live in a society that does so?

So, if we can relate to our minds and life being like that of the moon, and the moon without the light of the sun that shines upon it is just a dark Rock going round in circles in the darkness of space and at times it is observed as darkness and light when the sun shines its light upon it and without the sun it would not be seen, why do we not decide that we want to change that? It would be easy to compare the darkness and light of the moon to be to life and also the tree of knowledge of good and evil. The knowledge of good and evil would then have to be the thing that causes the problems in our minds, relationships and society and the way in which people are forced to live because people do not make the changes necessary for everyone to live in a better way, with love. We are all living our lives with the effects of the knowledge of good and evil and the knowledge of good and evil can give a hope for and desire for love but it can never give birth to it because it is not it, it can only reap what it sows, seeds of hurt, pain, suffering and division.

Now consider how the sun interacts with the moon. It shines its amazing love and life-giving light upon it, sometimes we can observe the sun and the moon both together in the daytime, when this happens it is as though the sun has allowed the moon into the light of day for it to join it, so that it can perhaps gain an appreciation of its love, life, light, day and ways. In doing so the sun may be able to embrace the moon and see all of its hurt through the trials of life. The sun will want the moon to change its understanding of itself so that it can be healed by it. If the moon does not accept this on those days, then it departs and goes about its journey again in the darkness, the darkness or space may well be considered or perceived by some as the tree of knowledge of good and evil. The sun sets, or the love ends through the failure of the moon to accept the love of the sun and again we see the hurt of the moon or the mind when the sun or love departs because it still, regardless of its refusal to accept it. But still It continues to shine its loving life-giving light upon it. Perhaps the moon sees the sun as a great big angry ball of fire just waiting to devour it and burn it? Maybe the moon does not understand the sun and that it just wants the moon to allow it in so that it can use its warmth to reignite the spark of love that it still has, so that it may be like itself, a life-giving being. How much more, light, love and warmth would we then have on Earth? And still, in life, people are given chance after chance to accept the Love or life or light of the sun. it really is an ongoing cycle. One that keeps us where we are without making progression and change as the loving beings that we were created to be, never actually getting anywhere and never changing, never experiencing the fulness of the Love that we could have.

Psalm 88:14 says, "why Lord do you reject me and hide your face from me?"

Perhaps the question should be... as we look into the mirror

..." why Lord do I reject your love and distance myself from you and recluse to the darkness where I suffer so much pain because I turn my face away from you?"

Was this psalm written by someone with the mind of the moon, someone who had been hurt and so desperately wanted to be loved by another but couldn't let go of the past experiences which was influencing their future life? if the question being asked is the Voice of Jesus himself then I am sure that he would be hurt

Let's look at the red stars... would all the suffering and pain that they carry and endure in life because their needs are not met cause them to become angry at times? Would they not be perceived to be shining a red, dangerous angry light into the lives of others, perhaps not because they would want to but because they have been forced to? And after realising that after shining that light into the lives of others would a good person not feel remorseful of their actions and caused to suffer even more? how much more then, do they need love and are deserving of it yet they still do not receive it?

The white stars, perhaps the ones that believe that they are perfect and that others are simply just unkind and deserve to suffer for their actions for they do not seek the love of the lord and so do not feel the need to help others. That being so, how much more do they need the love of the Lord so that they can help others?

Each star can be observed to go through what is called a stellar evolution on its journey in life, its colour changes over time with age, until the star either explodes as a supernova and dies, apparently the death of these stars exploding form dense neutron stars and black holes which trap light.

Is it not possible that it actually produces planets as well? They do indeed! Is it not possible that the black holes, which apparently nobody has seen is actually just another star? They are! A star that hides itself at times!

Look at planet earth and what we know about it, it has a molten core, is that not the sign, evidence and remnant of the thing that it once was before it cooled down? Do we not all live on this cooled down life-giving planet that works in what could be perceived by some as harmony with all the others?

We know that earth has a molten core, one that would look exactly like the sun, right at its centre!

We know that planet earth has a protective life-giving atmosphere all around it, the ozone, the atmosphere and the stratosphere... something that is far greater in size than the planet beyond the rocky surface, what a coincidence that this atmosphere looks rather like Saturn with its rings? Is it a coincidence?

Look at Neptune and the depths of colour and the variations of such colour in its blueness, how peculiar that the earth, covered with its oceans and the different depths of them can clearly be seen with such similar colours. Is it possible that Neptune is a reflection of the earth's ocean?

Venus and Mars, reddish brown and golden-brown coloured planets, how similar do those spherical objects look compared to the soil, Earth and rock that form on the outer sphere with its colours?

Are the stars, moons and planets not all then the same, but changed through experiences and time on the journey in life? And if we can all relate to them through the mirror of a telescope, perhaps conceive that we who walk the earth are rather like the earth and all have a fiery golden core of love at our centre then can't we all collectively choose to shine that light into the lives of others equally because we are all equal because we are all the same? What would happen to the celestial bodies we see in space should we change what we do on Earth? Would the appearance of the night sky change? Would the stars disappear should they be loved and ministered to, should they feel accepted and at home on the Earth? Would they all come back down to Earth, their home, as depicted in Armageddon? Is Armageddon perceived as through the eyes of man and an evil war a bad thing or is Armageddon as depicted through the eyes of Christ a loving thing, a good thing?

It can be whatever we choose for it to be!

Depending on who we choose to be!

If that be done then things certainly would change, they wouldn't go back to how things were, they would become what they are meant to be! The tree of knowledge would be no more. If we could do that and we looked through a telescope after we did that then what would happen? If we changed the colours of the stars and the journey that we currently perceive them to go through in their lifetime, I believe that rather than observing the sun, or love that is within us through a mirror, it would be in us and we would be in it and if we were to be in it then there would only be one colour, the colour of love, if it has one! For if the colour of the stars in the darkness of the night sky were to change, would they not change here on earth as well?

Perhaps we perceive the world in all of its colours because of these things? It is a beautiful place when observed in so much colour. But was it always like that or meant to be like that? I think not, for there is pain and suffering in the world and if it is pain and suffering that created so much colour and the bible speaks of a world with no more pain and no more suffering in the book of Revelation chapter 21 verses 1:4. If pain and suffering creates colour and it isn't meant to be that way then what if everyone was to accept the greatest of loves into their life? What colour would we see things then? Would it truly be Pure Gold living with the sun inside the sun or living with love and in love, for everyone to do so? The Bible does indeed also tell us in the book of revelation 22:5, and night will be no more. they will need no light of the lamp or sun, for the Lord God will be their light, and they will reign forever and ever! Perhaps Love is Colourless and has no colour, it is an invisible God Afterall, isn't it? Perhaps for some it may be!

So if love is not Golden in colour but is the refiner of Gold and silver, what must it be? A diamond! One of the strongest substances known to ever exist on the earth! One of the most expenses rocks on the earth, the less flawed and colourless they are, the more precious and treasured they are!

But only in the eyes of man.

The truth, may it be told, is that you can readily and easily purchase one of the greatest, most clear precious diamonds in the world for just a few pounds! Or if you wanted to I am sure the right person would just give you one for free!

A Bible! The thing that some people perceive as nothing more than a worthless lump of used coal!

In order to experience the fulness of God we need to draw closer to the sun or love for if we do not and we look into the distance, in the opposite direction, may our future be seen, Pluto, a small baron rock, host of no or little life, on its elliptical orbit around the sun, on its journey it appears to battle against millions or billions of others similar to itself as it passes through the Kuiper belt in order to get back closer to the sun, crashing and smashing getting hurt as it does so! Ooh the pain of such a journey! Rather like life!

Should we all not all want to live with the sun as our core and live in the sun together?

Was not the Ark of the Covenant covered in pure gold, and therefore its reflection and perception unto others as they observed it a beautiful golden reflection? If someone was to open the ark of the covenant and saw nothing in there, I would say to them, you are wrong, I see on the inside that which I saw on the outside, pure Gold. But for some, it may be in darkness with two pieces of "BROKEN" stone! Perhaps, similarly we are living on earth receiving life from our Sun in the sky and perhaps our sun is a black hole covered and the heat and colour that we see it to be is Gold, Fools Gold? Rather like the Ark of The Covenant if it was to be darkness inside with the tablet of truth that was broken into two and divided, and overlaid with Gold.

If that be the case then what would the Earth be? The Earth would be Love, we are on the Earth and therefore we are part of the earth and therefore we also are love. Will we all decide to love ourselves and heal the earth so that we can experience it in all of its fulness or will we continue to see it neglected as has been done for such a long time and end up as baron rocks with no life just floating around in the darkness of space. Or even worse, will we end up as the darkness of space itself, where there is no more light... dead!

What colour do you see in? Ask your own mind. Do you see things in love and unity or in darkness and division.

I see both and want to make things better, simply because I know the Love that Christ has for us.

I Have overcome, so have many others. Will you also?

This amazing creation that we experience and live in that is called life, it is beautiful, you just have to apply your mind to see the beauty of it, appreciate the moon for all that it is, to be able to realise that, our closest celestial object, a sign of who we are! We are the universe!

If we carry on the way that we are with pain and suffering then we will end up like the planets that roam around in space, abandoned and deserted with no star to support its life, a little Rock in the darkness with no love! How sad would that be?

But for a life with no more pain or suffering and no more tears as the bible promises, well, it is down to us as people to collectively want to change that so that we can have what is promised and that what appears to have been lost. An Eternal Life!

Do We Have the Power or Love or the Will To Change Or Do We Have To Wait To Be Changed or are we destined for one thing? If we genuinely do have free will then are we prepared to use it for the greater good?

Perhaps I was changed so that others did not need to be, so that they did not need to suffer because of evil or doubt as Jesus or Love Did and does. Or perhaps I just rediscovered who I truly am and accepted Christ.

The more that I focus on one aspect of Jesus the deeper my mind searches, the greater my unity with Jesus and also appreciation of Love and of course I change again.

Will you accept that his word is true and will you accept him also?

If you suffer, know that You are Loved and deserve much better, you deserve to know that you are Love and that you have already overcome because he has done that for us.

EVERYBODY DOES!

The Parable Of The Goats And The Sheep

Matthew 25 31-46

31 "When the Son of Man comes in his glory, and all the angels with him, he will sit on his glorious throne. 32 All the nations will be gathered before him, and he will separate the people one from another as a shepherd separates the sheep from the goats. 33 He will put the sheep on his right and the goats on his left.

34 "Then the King will say to those on his right, 'Come, you who are blessed by my Father; take your inheritance, the kingdom prepared for you since the creation of the world. 35 For I was hungry and you gave me something to eat, I was thirsty and you gave me something to drink, I was a stranger and you invited me in, 36 I needed clothes and you clothed me, I was sick and you looked after me, I was in prison and you came to visit me.'

37 "Then the righteous will answer him, 'Lord, when did we see you hungry and feed you, or thirsty and give you something to drink? 38 When did we see you a stranger and invite you in, or needing clothes and clothe you? 39 When did we see you sick or in prison and go to visit you?'

40 "The King will reply, 'Truly I tell you, whatever you did for one of the least of these brothers and sisters of mine, you did for me.'

41 "Then he will say to those on his left, 'Depart from me, you who are cursed, into the eternal fire prepared for the devil and his angels. 42 For I was hungry and you gave me nothing to eat, I was thirsty and you gave me nothing to drink, 43 I was a stranger and you did not invite me in, I needed clothes and you did not clothe me, I was sick and in prison and you did not look after me.'

44 "They also will answer, 'Lord, when did we see you hungry or thirsty or a stranger or needing clothes or sick or in prison, and did not help you?'

45 "He will reply, 'Truly I tell you, whatever you did not do for one of the least of these, you did not do for me.'

46 "Then they will go away to eternal punishment, but the righteous to eternal life."

....

Quite a scary ending, right? Love would never do that as love is what it says that it is.

So, who then is the son of man, what is his glory and his angels and what do they do by having them on his left and his right?

Well, if the son of man would have people on his left and his right and cause some to depart then that would certainly be causing division or divorce or separation, wouldn't it? Therefore, that action would be unkind and not of God, it would be considered Anti-Christ or evil. Therefore, the son of Man would be Considered as the love of man...certainly many people can relate to that in today's society. In experiences with personal relationships, the laying down of rules, things we can and cannot do in life.

So, who are the angels if the son of man comes with them? The son of man must be an angel, or many. If Our own Love or spirit leaves us so that we may be left with and discover the Love of the lord then the spirit that leaves us is not the holy spirit, but an angel, something that many people can be seen to relate to such as greed and selfishness etc.

But when we cast out or overcome these angels in our own minds we do not cease to exist, we discover who we are, the Love of the lord, The purest of loves, The Holy Spirit.

We realise that we do not need to invite the holy spirit in, but we simply need to accept it, that which is already in us. It is then that things begin to change in life.

If we accept these things then we accept Jesus, will everyone be willing to accept Jesus when the time comes so that they may have everything that they ever needed so freely or will they continue to deny Jesus and continue life on their own with so many struggles and hardships?

So, are the Angels actual beings as depicted in movies and books as we see in society today? The other aspect of the world or evil that estranges us so far from the truth about love?

Perhaps an angel is a person's own understanding of Love, their own way of Life, the thing that makes them a Lord, a Lord or a love that causes division be it because of doubt or unkindness rather than unity and joining together, the love of THE Lord, Jesus, the Love that everyone has and deep down wants and needs more of in all of its fullness. They are with the Lord but not the lord and still the Lord Loves them and gives them the opportunity to accept him.

And look at the Saints, was Saint George not depicted riding a horse and trampling over the head of a serpent? If it was his own love that he trampled on, the son of man being his own love, so that he could become a better person then great, in fact that is fucking amazing, he deserves to be called a saint. If someone sees the love of another to be the son of man rather than the son of God and they choose to trample on the head or someone else's love, then is that an action of THE Lord? Far from it! He does not force us to accept his Love, only the Son of Man would force you to accept their love. But even the saints, did they not also die in the end? Perhaps they grasped the concept of Love, but to what avail if they died in the end? Perhaps because not every tongue did confess that Jesus is Lord And Saviour of all, or that Jesus is Love and that Love can save all!

I don't believe that there is any significance in the character of people on the left in regards to their location, the same as the people on the right. Other than on the whole, we see that the love of man causes division, the love of man or the head of man that causes division, in this case by separating the goats from the sheep is represented by the head of the actual goat, an animal with two horns on its head. "Out of its one head or its one love came two" Division! This is not a love of God. If it is the Love of Man that causes so much division then it must surely be the love of man that can heal it and bring unity and peace for all. But only if Mankind, all of mankind accept that they are Love, can we find such unity in that book called the bible? Yes we can, it is challenging and hard as it says, but it is worth it in the end. For the reward is Love, Perfect Love!

Let me give you an example of modern-day Goats and sheep, unity and division. The House Of Commons, London, UK.

Right down the middle, seated in what does indeed appear to be a throne with two parties either side of him is the speaker of the house of Commons. Not knowing which side would be the goats we would have to test them by their fruits to see if their actions cause division or unity.

Generally, these two groups of people are the labour and conservative party. One party having the "apparent" power in the UK'S "apparent" Democracy depending on whether you are the speaker seated in the chair or looking at the speaker as you would perceive it if watching on television, the goats could be on the left or the right. To make decisions that affect the whole nation. The decisions that we see them make, do they bear fruit? Do they bear fruit for everyone or just some people? Also, what kind of fruit do they bear? Sweet enjoyable fruit or bitter fruit? Do they create division by bearing fruit for some and not others or do they bear fruit for everyone and is that fruit sweet for everyone and in their best interests and the interests of the planet and future generations?

The other side of the house of commons is known as the "opposition" they make their arguments because they want the power that the opposition has. They gain it, and then what? They do the same. They bear the fruit of Goats.

And The speaker of the house of Commons who sits in the apparent throne in the middle of these people. Would it not therefore be his role to join together these two groups of people with love and instruct them so that they can address the common interests of the people? Interests that benefit all. Yet we do not witness this at all, quite the opposite actually. We witness comments of humour that cause one group of people to become angry. We witness lack of Godly instruction. Doing nothing is the same as doing evil, it bears unkind fruit by allowing the prevalence of it.

Perhaps they do not know how to do such things, perhaps they are unqualified and incompetent as far as Gods standards go. I think it is true to say that because they do not taste their own fruit, they do not perceive their own actions in order to be able to comprehend their own Ark and take accountability for their own actions by cutting off the branches that do not bear fruit for they do not see that their own fruit is bitter. Their actions also are witnessed to be the head of a goat and their love of Man. It is therefore not a House of Commons but by its fruit, rather a House Of Goats. Very sad, very sad indeed when their actions and decisions cause suffering for the very people that they are supposed to represent and to make life better for. It could also be viewed as a house of angels, a Bottomless Pit of Serpents and eternal Darkness, or even a Synagogue of Satan.

How do I know such things? Because people with similar beliefs and ways of thinking that represent those beliefs

139

chose to cut off a branch of my own that was bearing fruit, very sweet and healthy fruit. Their actions in doing so were an act of evil, unkindness, or Anti-Christ, they came from a system that holds records of wrong forever.

But what a Good Question that we are faced with in that chapter of Matthew that we should all ask ourselves in relation to God, Love.

What did you do for Jesus?

One could indeed suggest that they suffered, and in suffering for Jesus by being kind or patient to an unkind person, they gained an understanding of Jesus. But would that be true that they suffered For Jesus, or would they have simply suffered because of Evil?

Both perceptions could be considered to be a truthful experience to the perceiver, but only one can be true. The perception that someone suffered for Jesus is a Lie, that person's mind has already fell back into prison, they have fallen into a trap. Evil would have succeeded if they believed such a thing.

Why? Because they would not have accepted Jesus in all of his fullness. The Fulness that shows that in belief he has the power to resurrect.

They would not have cherished the whole message and Love of Christ. And why? Because there is still evil in the world. And so, the world that we live in today must change, it needs to be restored and to be restored with love.

One could say that they provided food, drink, clothes and shelter for the financially poor and the needy. That would be and is considered an act of kindness. What if the people that they provided those things to had a mind or head or Love of division, did they not also provide to Love and Evil? Is giving to those causes and charity's itself not an act of division that comes from a mind of division? Rather like putting a sticking plaster on a wound instead of dealing with the problem that caused the wound in the first place? It is an example of a lesser love. One that we can all relate to at times and one that comes from not accepting Jesus in fulness. Who is anyone else to take that away from anyone that does the will of God, other than Evil?

Evil or doubt and fear which comes from the knowledge of right and wrong, or rules. These are what create such things that give life or love to life and death, the thing we can all relate to. Only love can give birth to love, the thing we all want and desire. If rules stop or prevent us from doing so, in any way shape or form, which they do, then shouldn't we break those rules to bring about the greater good?

What prevents the government from loving? Rules!

Go against the grain, do not conform to the pattern of the world or evil so that in doing so you will be transformed by the renewal of your mind! Do not do this so that the pain that it may have caused you will be directed back at them but having gained Love, give them Love so that they themselves do not have to suffer the pain that you have.

Be bold and courageous…. In Love!

Matthew 6:1-4 says, Truly I tell you, they have received their reward in full. But when you give to the needy, do not let your left hand know what your right hand is doing, so that your giving may be in secret. Then your father, who sees what is done in secret, will reward you.

We should give freely to all and not just where there is a need. And that is where the action of making decisions for the benefit of all comes into it. We should not think of our actions when we are giving and whether or not it is right or wrong and whether we are giving to someone of a mind of division and we should not ask ourselves if this is okay or not to do so. But, what greater of a love would there be if there was no need to give and all were to share in pure Love?

The purpose of making decisions for all with the Love of the Son Of Man that we see now will fail, because many of the ways of society today revolve around one thing…money.

If the truth is that money is the root of all evil then surely, we must make a society that revolves around something else in the absence of money... LOVE!

I and anyone else could choose to say that for Jesus I loved myself, that I am Jesus I could choose to be kind, patient, forgiving of myself, etc and myself only. I could choose to misinterpret the scripture that says "Jesus will never leave me" and as such choose not to be kind and patient to others. If others looked at me, they could then perceive me to be a selfish person by only thinking of myself and they would be correct to do so because my fruit would be very bitter. If I was to do that then I would also be being unkind to myself and suffer the affliction caused to my mind by the suffering that I see of others in society each day. As would anyone else with a love for others, Empathy. So that would be feeding Jesus and Evil also and that would not be done for Jesus or Love.

So, what then would be the point in drawing near to listen, allowing our speech to be fruitful all the time, being patient with evil people, holding no records of wrong, not boasting in our unkindness, being doers of the word and not just listeners or speakers of it?

Would these things not just be meaningless?

Ecclesiastes 2 verses 11-12 even portray that the reflection of man knowing Jesus is meaningless.

It does indeed say, what can someone who inherits Love do that has not already been done?

Is it possible to do a new thing?

Of course, it is!

The bible also says this in the book of Isiah, it says "Behold, I am doing a new thing, do you not perceive it?"

I already did a new thing in a sense and the Lord said to me... "I have never had a star do that to me before!"

Now if we are to do unto others as we would have done to ourselves and I did that to The Lord then what would The Lord have to have done to me? He Loved me and in doing so he changed me, he corrected my path and showed me who I am.

I do so many things that I am not sure what it is that I did that caused the Lord to say such a thing so I may not be able to discern exactly what it was but if I have to take a shot in the dark then I would have to say that it was this.... This one time, I perceived Jesus in such a way that when I expressed it through my own creativity it came about like this... "I LOVE JESUS BECAUSE JESUS IS A DICK" and it is true, Jesus is a complete, pure, total, absolute DICK! He is an absolute Bell end!

Not only is he a Dick but he is a Dick HEAD!"

And guess what the best thing about that is?

He cannot chastise me for that, for if he does then he is not who he says he is and as such he has to love me for it and appreciate my growth and understanding of him by accomplishing such a great thing, doing a new thing when everything is apparently meaningless! Therefore, I have proven that not everything is meaningless and love does grow and that Jesus is alive!

Is that not bold and courageous?

Was Eve actually Evil, or in asking the question "did God actually say do not eat the fruit of this tree?" Did she not demonstrate that she doubted by the action of questioning?

If Adam and eve represent both trees then surely, we should help Eve by showing her love by allowing her to overcome her doubt so that she could be healed? Rather than being male and female, did Adam and Eve not represent the thinking of the mind of mankind, male and female?

We also have a story of Abrahams wife Sarah who was without child, she was baron, was this a female that could not have children or a person who because of doubt was seen to be evil and then neglected because of this and was then without child or without love given to her by others? That being so, did she, like a star, find it hard to share love and give love to others? Was

Abraham, the one with two wives, or two loves, a goat?
Did he have a mind of division?

These are all great questions and ones that I ask myself when I read my bible, it allows me to help others in life and gives me an appreciation for Jesus and the amazing things that he has to offer everyone.

We could also write books for or about Jesus; the bible instructs us to do such things, also different aspects of things. But unless they are books about Love then would that be his will? What then Is the Purpose Of These Things?

Of course, it has to be his will, for everything is about Love, for love is everything, Love can only get better!

We can not make things better if the things that need to be made better are not addressed, that is perfectly rational thinking!

To raise awareness of Jesus, in a way that people can relate to, understand him and want more of him.

So rather than seek the son of man on an individual basis in life, shouldn't we seek the son of God and use that to help the son of man so that that things can get better?

Not many books, even Christian books do such things and indeed, they could do things so much better, so could I, because they are written with a mind tainted

IT ALL STARTED WITH AN
ARGUMENT WITH TWO SIDES TO
THE STORY!

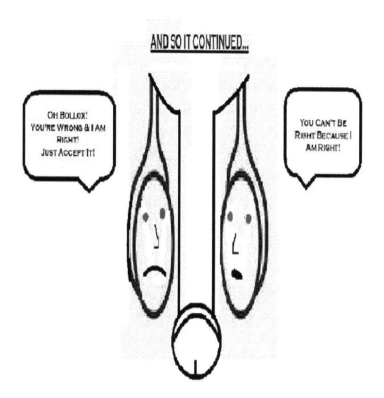

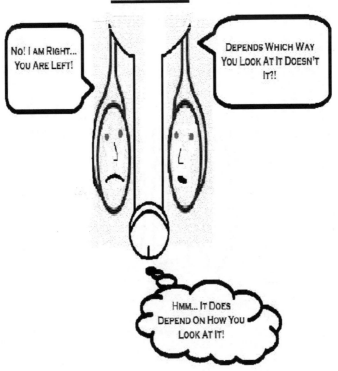

154

...Until!

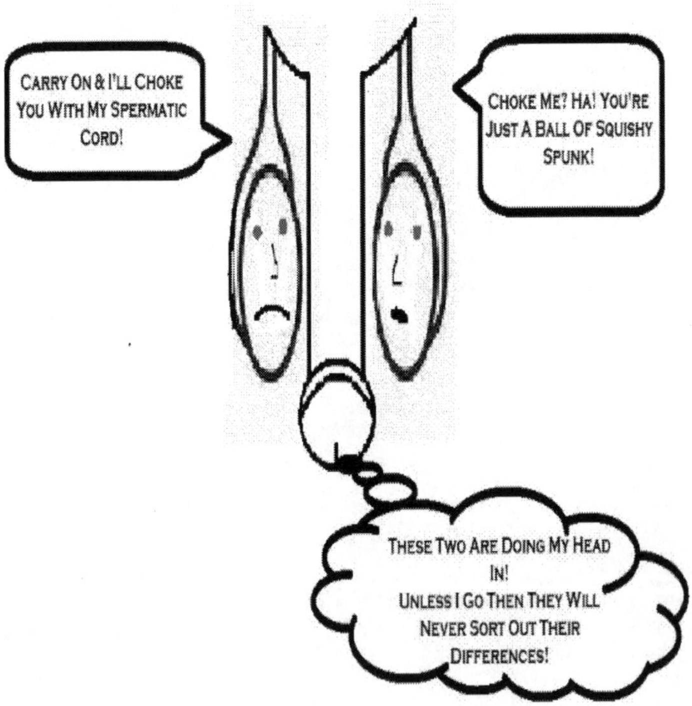

Carry On & I'll Choke You With My Spermatic Cord!
Choke Me? Ha! You're Just A Ball Of Squishy Spunk!
These Two Are Doing My Head In!
Unless I Go Then They Will Never Sort Out Their Differences!

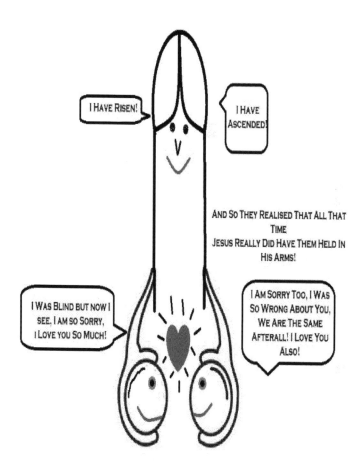

**AND SO THEY REALISED THAT ALL THAT TIME
JESUS REALLY DID HAVE THEM HELD IN
HIS ARMS!**

Well my child, you certainly did get me on that one, you did
curse me & praise me at the same time.
yes you did do a new thing, you created a new word that
best describes life at times, the thing that I work
throughout!

Do not worry about what others may think, go against the
grain, be bold and courageous! If they do not like it then
they can always look into the mirror to see that it is Good!

I was with you when you wrote it was I not? I am
Omnipotent and Omnipresent, in fact I knew that you would
do it before were even born, I ordained it for you!

That's what people don't seem to understand, they think its
okay to lay down rules for others that restrict knowledge of
my true love. The one that you know because you loved me
and I loved you in the beginning!

.....Lest We Forget.....

I FUCKING LOVED IT MY SON!
HAHAHAHA!

And so, the seeds that were needed to be sown were sown and all began to come back home, if they wanted to.

Jesus would come to you completely with all of his love but he would only give that to you if you allowed him to do so.

His love for us is in the mirror, or the bible...go take a look at it, if you read something that you do not like in there then examine your mind and see how you can grow in love.

How great would it be for two seeds of love to grow together from the start? That's when people would be ready for the perfect Marriage!

That was the story of the CURAISE, how I managed to turn something that was perceived as some to be unkind or evil, into something that was kind and loving to give praise to Jesus, Our God!

Isn't that what God wants us all to do?

Although I made a new word, "Curarise" and a new cartoon that has likely never been seen before...did I really do a new thing? Or did I just appreciate the love that I received from Jesus and express it in my own way, if that be so then that certainly has been done before.

Perhaps I did do a new thing, perhaps I just did something differently....no, I did both, and I am unique.

Just as you are, the reader. We all do things differently, you are Unique, and yet we are all the same.

But remember this, you are precious, you are treasured, you are loved, you are love! We all are!

One good question to ask is this, can we Curaise someone else, or do we Curaise ourselves?

<u>RANDOM</u>

This chapter is just about Random waffle and thoughts of someone reflecting upon the content of a book that they have written because to write about Love in its entirety would take so much time that it would be impossible to complete such a thing. This also is true!

That's not to say that I won't want to or have the opportunity to write one again in future though.

So here we go, just a few pages of random thoughts and crazy things...

ODES

(One Drop Every Seed)

Some people say that I only got one drop of the ocean.

If that is so then that was all that I needed, one drop changed me.

It also changed the Ocean, for that one drop that I consumed was taken from the ocean and the ocean was one drop less. Because the ocean was one drop less, it to was changed, it became a completely different ocean.

One Drop

One Seed

That drop was a seed that grew, and the ocean knew, that one day that love would come back Anew.

Because I would learn to love, every part of you!

The drop of life, the blood of Christ the seed of Love that brings the spirit of the Dove.

How Far Must We Go

How far must we go, this far and no further.

How far is that, as far as you went?

If you went further than I, then I must go further!

How deep must we go? Must we stay in the shallow?

If you went to the bottom, then I too must follow!

How high must we go? To the darkness of space?

If you are there then I will come to that place.

In which direction, north, east, south or west?

I have an idea; I know what is best.

I will just stay here, in your peace, your rest.

But if you ever need me, just call out my name,

And I will call yours, our love is the same.

Judgement Day

They say that you should never judge a book by its
cover,

Did you expect to find Satan but instead got Gods
Lover?

Didn't like what you read?

Then go try another!

But didn't you like it, did you read something horrible?

Then go read the bible!

Take a look in that mirror or glance at the stars,

See the pain of the wars,

Or the beauty of Mars!

See the beauty of love, or unkindness that tars.

Do whatever you like, but remember this,

Do it with Love, and don't take the piss!

Give to another just what they deserve,

for that which we judge, will also be served.

So isn't it best to always serve love,

Then all can find rest, in the spirit of the Dove.

Never Judge a book by its cover, for inside it, you may find your lover.

Sky

Interesting, taken aback, amazed?

The question I have is, are you Curaised?

If your mind was the sky, then has it been raised?

Perhaps it's been peeled back,

Theres no need for Flak,

Appreciate the beauty that lies deep within,

And know that whatever battle you're in,

You will win!

For it was already won,

By Gods only Son

So we don't have to, Feel down, beaten and blue.

Are we living in that promise, me, and you?

Let's take it, let's hold it, and never let go,

Let us do the will of God, let us all Sow!

TEACHING, SHARING AND CARING

Teaching.

Luke 2 41:52 tells us about the boy Jesus.

When Jesus was sat in the temple courts with the Teachers, he told his mother and father "did you not know that I had to be in my father's house?"

It is therefore my understanding and belief that Love was with the Teachers and that the mind of a teacher is also a house of God and that to teach about Love is Good and Kind, it is Love. Yet so many things in live are taught, but where is the teaching of Love? Do we have to learn through life because it is not taught anymore?

What if we were taught about it? Would life then be so much better, pleasurable and enjoyable?

Certainly!

How we teach is of great importance, many people say that the bible is useful for teaching, for reproof, correcting, and training in righteousness. But if the end result or harvest is what we sow, then isn't it better to teach about love and love only? If we teach about reproof and correcting, then wont we reap a harvest of correction?

I hope that I have been able to do so in writing this book and sharing my own treasure with you as food and I hope that these seeds grow to bear fruit and bring about change.

We are also instructed that not many of us should become teachers, my brothers, for you know that we who teach will be judged with greater strictness.

If that be so and I have made a mistake then correct me also but know that I have tried my best and wrote this book with a pure heart, or at least, as pure a heart as possible considering the trials I have endured and my current circumstances as well as my want for a better world and restoration and with an intention for helping others in their lives and struggles, I also wish for it to help me, not for any selfish or unkind reason but because I so desperately need others to repent and feel the healing and love, Freedom through Forgiveness.

I want to live in a world where I see a smile on everyone's face, a genuine smile! I do not want to be made to feel sad by seeing others struggle, sad and unhappy.

Let's make things better!

Sharing.

It is good to share, and so, if you have enjoyed reading this book, have been helped by it, been built up by it, felt touched by it, been changed by it, been encouraged to read a bible in a different way or even buy a bible for the first time or have just really enjoyed it, then please, tell a friend about it and recommend it to them. Even better, tell all of your friends about it or better still, buy copies of it to give to them as free gifts!

I hope that you found the food contained in this book as fine as treasure and as wealthy as riches of Gold & Silver with lots of little Gemstones. At the price that it is per head I can guarantee you that you will struggle to be able to purchase food of this calibre at any restaurant anywhere in the world for such a low price.

My Journey into the Ark has been a very difficult and time consuming one as I am sure that from the contents, those who understand will agree.

Caring.

If you care about others, as I do, and have been inspired by any of the content of my book then perhaps consider trying to write your own in order to help others. Others that may have been through similar experiences as yourself, in a kind way that will strengthen and support them and build them up, in a way that allows them to understand things, a way that gives them a hope and a possibility of a better future.

Its good to write, as hard as it may be. At times of writing, I have felt that I wasn't ready to do so because of how certain topics of this book made me feel but I did it and I overcame those feelings which were in my mind that had been caused by others from past experiences, I conquered, because I persevered! I had to, and I do it every day, with the hope of things getting better.

Writing about these things is also something that Jesus wants us to do because it brings about a revelation of Love and who Jesus is. It allows us to learn about problems so that they may be addressed and things made better.

The bible actually tells us to write on many occasions.

Hopefully, One day, Humanity may be able to stand and shout "WE ARE JESUS!" Because in and on that day, I truly believe that he will be with us!

I myself am not perfect and I know I make mistakes at times; I know that because it hurts my brain! I feel divided! I make mistakes in respect of, I could do better, I could be more patient and kinder etc and I am sure that many people could, but as long as there are always problems in society then humanity will always have problems, it makes sense to find solutions to problems, selfless loving solutions that benefit everyone.

The misconception of many is that problems and things will sort themselves out but problems don't do that if nobody addresses them, we need to sort things out together in unity with Love at the core and make things better!

I just hope that in writing this book I have been able to convey my experiences and understanding of the bible to others in a simple, truthful and understandable way that is relevant for today. In a way that will bring people together and makes things better so that people may be more open minded, understanding and compassionate of and towards others which may help to take away people's pain in some respect, until the day of forgiveness comes. If we all do that then we have succeeded, I hope that I get to see the fruit of such actions of forgiveness so that my own mind can be made better and healed to the extent that I am able to enjoy life more.

Thank you, the reader, and thankyou Jesus for All that you do, have done and are about to do in future. If we can not yet have all things made New as you promise right now, then may we be renewed and things be made better for those that need it.

My final thoughts are these…. If there is anything in this book that you do not agree with, then I really do not give a fuck, it isn't perfect and it doesn't say "Holy Bible" of the front fucking cover, does it, you complete, absolute, total fucking dick! You are a pure fucking bell end!

And if you think that this book is fucked up, well that's because the world and society is fucked up and it fucked me up also, but at least I Love God and have a sense of humour! Ha ha!

The End.

Or is it?

Now, Knowing the truth, that we are all just a bunch of absolute dick heads, will we learn to look after ourselves and do things that bring pleasure into our lives in a better way and be responsible stewards of our Love?. Do we have what it takes to accept the hand of God and become absolute fucking wankers so that we can all reach the point of climax together and consume all those seeds that we sow from doing that, the seeds that are actually leaves and for healing?

THE HAND OF GOD!

But there are two sides to every story... some of us are introverts and some of us are extroverts! Look I can prove it!

Female reproductive system

Cock and balls on the inside = An Introvert

Male Reproductive system

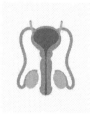

Cock and balls on the outside = Extrovert

We are all the same but different!

And So, Men and women everywhere throughout the universe accepted Love, they accepted that in the absence of their appearance of being female and male in physical appearance that God made man and that man was Love and that the seed of Man was love, because everyone realised that they were Children of love and wanted more and more love.

They learned to do things that brought the fruit of the spirit into their lives, they ate everything because everything was Love and there was no more rotten fruit because they learned to be kind to each other and not physically and mentally hurt each other anymore, the pain in their bodies disappeared because of this and there was no more tears and no more suffering because they had been taught and learned how to use Love for the benefit of all, for its greater good and Man and woman lived on earth happily ever after.

Printed in Great Britain
by Amazon